FROM DOING TO LEADING

"This is by far one of the best leadership books I have read. I have been in a manager's role for a couple different companies and was recently promoted to a manager role with the company I'm with now. I feel like this book gives you a play by play of how to build and run a team and be a great leader. I highly recommend this book to anybody who is a manager. I plan on reading this book throughout my career as a guide."

Graham Whitlock,
Regional Account Development Manager for
Caliber Collision Centers

"This is a must read, especially for those in and related to the industry. Every chapter left me eager to read the next. John eloquently simplifies the concepts of neurochemistry into applicable principles. I was quick to use this book as a training tool for our entire leadership team. Each of my managers were able to clearly relate to the struggles and I have seen many positive results from the easily implemented tools. If you are a doer or a leader you will see yourself in this book and be eager to make the transition."

Nick Edwards,
Owner Car Center Collision & Mechanical

"I'll be honest I'm not a huge reader and have yet to find a book that translates into the body shop until I found this book. The book relays the struggles and the opportunities that we come across every day in the body shop industry. If you're moving from a doer to a leader in the near future I highly recommend the book. Wish I had the opportunity to read the book back when I was promoted to a center manager years ago."

Daniel Stallard,
Regional Vice-President, Caliber Collision

"*From Doing to Leading* helps you learn how to boost the untapped potential of your most precious commodity: *your people.* I have shared this book with my team and have seen fantastic results. Even after nearly 30 years in the business, I find the insights in this book to be phenomenal. I can only imagine how much it could have influenced the younger version of me and certainly will help build team development in our shops from here on in. This book is the perfect read for those of us "nut and bolts car guys and gals" who put in the work every day."

Charles M. Drake,
Chief Operations Officer of Classic Collision

"I purchased this book to learn how to lead more effectively and have a deeper understanding of human behavior. After receiving and reading the book it was a no brainer, I provided all of our instructors and operations teammates a copy at our training facility. The information was nicely explained and it was easy to comprehend. Our instructors have seen the positive results in our students when they put to use the knowledge they received from this book. This book provides the "WHY" behind human behavior. It's a must have if you are leading a small group or a class of 20 people. I highly recommend this book if you are in a leadership role or you work with a team."

Douglas Willberg,
Director of Technical Training for
Caliber Collision Centers

FROM DOING TO LEADING

FROM DOING TO LEADING

Your Guide for Inspiring People on the Front Lines

JOHN M. STUEF
& AMY D. BRADSHAW, PHD

DEDICATION

This book is written for frontline leaders and workers.

For them, obstacles are simply hurdles that they will overcome.

Frontliners are the ones who do the work and get the job done!

TABLE OF CONTENTS

*"Leadership and Learning Are
Indispensable to Each Other."*

JOHN F. KENNEDY

AT THE END of 2017, the Detroit Lions football team was sitting on back-to-back seasons with nine wins and seven losses. If you're a fan of the Lions and a native of Detroit like me, you know such a thing was a pretty big deal. I remember going to a Lions game when I was a kid with my Dad. They were losing 38-0 when we left in the third quarter. That pretty much summed up being a Lions fan when I was growing up. To put it in perspective, the Lions have been playing professional football since 1930 and are the only team in their division yet to play in a Super Bowl. So when we finished nine and seven, two years in a row, loyal Lions fans had a reason for hope. We had a good team and a strong foundation. The owners seemed to think we just needed the right coach to lead them.

The New England Patriots have a superb football organization—they have five Super Bowl wins in ten Super Bowl appearances. When the Lions announced they were hiring Matt Patricia, a long-term assistant coach with the Patriots, I thought, *Wow! I'm excited to watch someone take our team to the next level and maybe our first Super Bowl.* The Lions had all the talent in place, and even though Patricia had never been a head coach, he had done a phenomenal job laying out the Patriot's defensive strategy and carried a well-earned reputation as someone who understood the strategy of the game. He was a proven doer.

Patricia took over the Lions as head coach in 2018 and proceeded to lead our team to a 6-and-10 season. It was the Lions' first losing season in three years. What happened? Patricia had been with a winning organization for more than ten years. He had three Super Bowl rings. How could a guy with a proven track record as a doer post a losing record as a leader? Well, here's the thing about going from doing to leading: Patricia's performance as a head coach was not going to be measured by his expertise for designing plays. He was going to be judged on his ability to inspire his entire team to bring their best on game day. He needed to make the transition from thinking like a doer to thinking like a leader.

I read an article that mentioned Patricia's habit of showing up as late as ninety minutes to his scheduled press conferences. He would give excuses such as his schedule was very busy. But this pattern also showed up in his interactions with his players. One ex-player commented that the coach was frequently late to team meetings as well. What became quite apparent to me from the article was Patricia had a lot of growth to do in the leadership department. Like all of us who start off as accomplished doers, he needed guidance to become a leader.

If Patricia understood that coming late to meetings sent his team a terrible signal, if he understood the *why* behind good leadership practices, then he could have applied this knowledge and become a more effective leader. His actions show a failure to put much thought into how his behavior conveyed his priorities to his team—one of the first lessons of leadership is self-awareness. As Tom Landry, the incredibly successful head coach of the Cowboys in the 1980s, said, "Leadership is a matter of having people look at you and gain confidence, seeing how you react. If you're in control, they're in control." Can you picture Landry showing up late for meetings and giving weak excuses?

When I first became a manager, I tried to drive achievement by pushing my team. I was a hard-driving boss who demanded results. Today, I clearly see the pitfalls of that method. Through my own life experiences, I have come to appreciate that the best way to lead people isn't by pushing them, but by tapping into their internal motivation. As I reflect on my career, I would have done a lot better and had a lot more success sooner if I had a "how-to-manage" book that fit my place on the front line. Most of the books out there seem to be geared toward the educated, white-collar, executive-level jobs. I didn't find those books to be all that relevant for a guy like me who was running a body shop. I needed a book on leading people from the ground level. A book like the one now in your hands. This book is co-authored by Dr. Amy Bradshaw, who has a PhD. I like to say I have a PhD as well, but mine stands for Poor, Hungry and Determined. Our goal is to bring you this guide for using human behavior to inspire your team and make every doer a leader.

NATURAL BORN LEADER

"Leaders Are Not Born, They Are Made."

VINCE LOMBARDI

WELCOME TO A different type of leadership book.

This book is for those of us who work with our hands, get dirty, and gut it out on the front lines every day. I wrote this book from my point of view—someone who picked up a lot of what he knows from the school of hard knocks. I didn't write this book for "executives" interested in climbing the corporate ladder while wearing a suit and tie. I wrote it for people I call "doers"—those of us who have spent a lot of time building things, fixing things, and writing estimates, but now find ourselves in a position needing to figure out how to lead people. I bet you're a person who gets stuff done, and I bet you like the feeling of accomplishment that comes from doing a task well. If you picked up this book, it's likely you were just promoted to management or decided to start your own business. You've earned recognition as a top performer or struck out on your own. First off, congratulations!

Chances are, though, as a "doer," you haven't put a lot of thought into how to lead people. The truth is the ones doing the work are usually occupied with a single task or set of tasks and don't have to worry about managing other people around them. The doers are focused on the best way to get their job completed. For them, taking a bird's eye view of tying together multiple tasks in an efficient workflow has always been the manager's job. When you transition from being a doer, the one performing the task—like fixing the car, writing the estimate, or setting the pipe—to being the one leading others, you're going to find that you need a different set of skills.

Often, after years of being a hands-on person, the biggest thing you miss is the feeling of doing it yourself.

You might also find you really miss the days when you didn't have to handle all the responsibilities. Depending upon your position, you'll soon realize that you're the one who takes the heat from the unhappy customer, the disgruntled workers, and the boss questioning why your team isn't performing. Yup, it all lies on you—you're the go-to guy. You might start resenting having to deal with all of the problems. You might feel like blaming your disengaged or missing-in-action team members who don't seem to really care. You might start thinking, *These guys are making me look bad*. You might start to feel like you can't trust anyone to get the job done, so you have to do it all yourself again. Or, maybe you've been a manager for some time, but you feel burned-out and frustrated by your team's lack of motivation and performance, plus you might have experienced a high turnover rate among your team members. The harder you push, the less effective you and your team become. Do any of these situations sound familiar? Well, they were very familiar to me when I was making the transition from doer to leader.

I think a lot of managers get stuck here and become frustrated. As a leader, your performance is measured by your team's performance, not your individual accomplishments. That's not how it was when you were a doer. While the transition from doer to leader is difficult, with the right tools, you too can become an exceptional leader. You've already moved up from a doer, someone who completes one task or a set of tasks, to a person who now needs to delegate these tasks to others. To do this well, you will need to start thinking about what motivates people and how to inspire them to do the tasks you used to do yourself. That's what this book is about: methods to help you tap into human nature to get the best from your team.

How many times have you heard someone use the phrase "natural-born leader"? Many people believe a person arrives on this earth equipped to be a leader, but I dispute that 100 percent. Leadership, like many things we do, is a learned skill. Consider a newborn human baby. There's no animal on the planet more needy or self-involved. Let's face it: babies do not have a lot of self-awareness. The key to great leadership is appreciating that it's all about "we" and not all about "me." Successful leadership centers on service to others and babies are all about service to themselves. So, no, there aren't a whole lot of natural-born leaders. We teach and guide our offspring how to care for and respect others. Likewise, leadership qualities are learned and developed. That being said, everyone has the capability to acquire more self-awareness and gain these qualities. No one is born a leader, but we can all become one.

In this first chapter, we will introduce four important points, some of which we will cover more in-depth in future chapters.

1. As a doer, you have the ability to become a great leader.
2. Leadership offers you a great opportunity to improve people's lives.
3. Great leaders inspire; poor leaders push.
4. The skills to become a great leader require an understanding of human behavior.

ARE YOU A CHICKEN OR A PIG?

Leadership, like most things, improves with experience and intention. The more you learn and practice good leadership techniques, the better leader you will become.

I recently talked to a group of center managers to roll out a new leadership guide. I said, "Before we start this morning, I want each of you to stand up, introduce yourself to the group, tell us how long you've been a leader at your center and then identify yourself as a chicken or a pig." After a few chuckles from the group, I explained that the pig and the chicken were an analogy about the difference between involvement and commitment. I said, "If you had bacon and eggs for breakfast this morning, the chicken was involved and the pig was committed."

Commitment is the starting point for great leadership. If you're not 100 percent committed to your team's safety and growth; your company's mission, vision and purpose; and your own personal development, then you need to rethink your desire to be a leader. Just like our offspring, who are not born knowing how to care and respect others, we need knowledge and guidance to develop as leaders. I once had a clinical psychologist explain to me that when people get stressed, they regress to an early childhood behavior to get their needs met. In other words, when babies are first born, they cry when they need something. Babies learn that they get what they want with this behavior. As adults, when we cry, yell, or scream, we are reaching back into our earliest emotional toolbox to get our needs met. As a baby, crying might be considered our first persuasion technique. With age and maturity, we utilize better emotional tools as we grow our interpersonal relationship tool set.

The same goes for leadership. Developing as a leader is a journey and requires personal reflection and self-awareness. Just as we mature emotionally from babies to adults, we advance in our careers from doers to leaders.

In this book, I am going to provide techniques for you to use so you can become a more successful leader using the lessons I have picked up along my way. Looking back on my career, I see how I progressed and expanded my tools to improve interpersonal relationships and leadership qualities. At the start, I had no appreciation of human behavior and no skills for managing people—I understood nothing about human behavior. Later, I bullied my way through owning and running my business. It wasn't until later in life, when I stepped away from the rat race and sought my own personal growth, that I came to see the huge benefits of using the techniques I will outline for you.

HOW NOT TO LEAD

HERE'S A NOTABLE example. During my first job as a manager of a ski rental service in Mayberry State Park in Michigan, I hired and then proceeded to fire my ex-wife (she actually became my wife and then my ex-wife sometime later). We were working out of a barn, and I told her she needed to sweep the place to keep the area clean. She asked, "Why, it's a barn?" My response was, "Because I said so, that's why and if you don't, you're fired." I bet you're not surprised that she refused and, well, I fired her. Team retention is critical and I wasn't exactly off to a great start. I had no clue how to inspire the people working for me. When I opened my first body shop in Detroit, I hadn't learned much more about human behavior. I hired my younger brother. When he quit three months later, he called my mother and told her I was the worst boss he had ever worked for. Moreover, my brother declared, "He's just like Dad!" Ouch. To say I was failing to learn and understand how to lead would be a gross understatement.

I can appreciate now that my leadership skills back then were based on my Dad's way of leading our family. He was a disciplinarian and his rules were non-negotiable. If you take a moment to reflect on your methods for leading a team, you'll likely find they were learned from your family. I had fashioned my leadership skills at work through the prism of my Dad's method for running the household. I was a bully as a leader. In my defense, just like most of us, thrust into a management position for the first time, I had no formal training in running a business or managing people. I had no real idea how to lead the people under me, let alone run a successful business, create a healthy, productive work environment, or nurture an engaged, inspired team.

As my career progressed and I took on larger teams of people, my management style evolved in some ways. In the middle of my career, I would describe my style as "set the goals and push your people to meet them." I was a people-pusher or even a cattle-driver. The phrases I would associate with this leadership style are: "stay on top of your team," "drive the team towards the goal," "push your people." People are not cattle. And you make no friends thinking of them or treating them this way. Think about how it feels to be physically pushed by someone. It's not a great feeling, is it? While I did have some career success at this time, it was very stressful for myself and my team. No one involved was having any fun.

So here's my first leadership tool for the toolbox: don't fall into the trap of using tactics to push team performance using external motivation as a driver. Motivation simply means you are pushing your team to perform. People rarely put all their energy into performing tasks for someone else when they're pushed. The short-term success that can come from pushing almost always leads to team member burn out and turnover. Phenomenal results happen when you use the methods I will share to light your team's internal fire of inspiration. My two decades of leading people using "motivation" or pushing them to perform never came close to the success of a team focused on a mission driven from an internal sense of purpose. Perhaps most surprising for me was the amazing sense of gratification I found in watching an inspired team work together.

THE REWARDS OF BEING A GOOD LEADER

I REMEMBER WHEN I first became a manager, transitioning from being a body technician, my boss at the time told me that I would miss the feeling of instant gratification that comes with working on my own projects. I was a doer and I felt a lot of satisfaction from completing a project. "When you fix a car, you see immediate results," he said. "When you manage people, you don't get that daily feeling of fulfillment—it's a monthly or yearly reward based on the financial performance of your department, shop or even company."

I disagree with that and would argue that great leaders can get immense satisfaction on a daily basis by watching their team bring their best. A team member who feels trusted, encouraged and successful is an incredible source of "instant gratification." When you see the very best in your people, I believe they will see the very best in themselves.

A recent study sheds some light on the importance of being a leader in the workplace. People were asked how they felt about their boss. Those who indicated their relationship with their immediate supervisor was better described as "a partner" than "a boss" reported a major increase in life satisfaction.

I want you to recognize that your position as a manager leading people has afforded you an amazing opportunity to make a huge impact on people's lives. You can choose to develop an inspired team who enjoys their day, their time at work, and their overall life satisfaction, or you can choose to be a controlling manager who pushes his team to produce (i.e. me in my early, misguided leadership days). I promise you that having an engaged team who works together is much more rewarding than being in charge of a stressed-out team consisting of miserable workers. As leaders, we all want to help create a nurturing, positive place for people to walk into every morning. But how do we go about doing that? It's not surprising that you might be feeling a little overwhelmed to be in a leadership position for the first time. You might feel a good bit of pressure to be a good leader but unsure where to find the tools to help you accomplish that.

I have been told on several occasions, "John, you're a natural-born leader." I never quite knew what that even meant. A large company once hired me to take over a body shop that was underperforming—for this book, we're calling this shop JMS Collision. This was at a time when I had just spent a good deal of effort researching human nature and leadership techniques. I was excited to use some of my newfound knowledge in a real-life setting. Before I walked in the door, JMS Collision had never exceeded $800,000 a month in sales and frequently failed to make a plan. In addition, the shop had a terrible customer satisfaction rating. I set a goal in my mind for this shop to earn $1 million a month in sales consistently and to excel in customer satisfaction with an engaged workforce. After three months of leading the store, I witnessed first-hand the power of the inspirational methods I am going to share with you in this book. When we came up on that first month in which our $1 million goal was in sight, everyone believed we could accomplish it. You could feel the excitement and the electricity in the air. Our entire team worked late into the evening the final day of the month as we closed in on our target for the first time. When we hit the $1 million mark, the incredible feeling of accomplishment was a wonderful thing to share with that great group of people. For me, I had a truly humbling appreciation for the power of engagement to inspire people. I had taken the people in this store from being a group of down-trodden, discouraged individuals to a successful team working together to break sales records with exceptional customer service. Am I a natural born leader? No—just like you, I am a doer who became a leader.

CHAPTER WRAP-UP

EACH AND EVERY one of us can be a great leader when given the proper insight and tools. To be an inspirational leader, it's very helpful to understand the science behind human behavior. In the next chapter, I'm going to share with you what I have learned about neurochemistry—why humans respond the way they do to stress, encouragement, engagement and reward.

You might be thinking, *neurochemistry*? That's way out of my wheelhouse. But trust me, if a guy like me can understand and use this information, so can you. As a leader, you're going to be in a position to control the release of neurochemicals to influence your team's behavior. We will also discuss the power of words, body language and persuasive techniques for building rapport and team engagement. We will touch on the importance of core values in the workplace and a proven method for helping you and your team implement processes. We will then revisit my experience taking over the under-performing JMS Collision, and I will explain step-by-step how I used my techniques to achieve the amazing results at that store. I will give you a point-by-point recap of how I inspired the people there to truly engage, work together and perform at the top of their game. To start, remember there are no natural-born leaders, but we all have a potential great leader inside us. Also, don't forget that leaders inspire, while managers control.

CHAPTER 2
THE SCIENCE BEHIND HUMAN BEHAVIOR

*"If Your Actions Inspire Others to Dream
More, Learn More, Do More and Become
More, You Are a Leader."*

JOHN QUINCY ADAMS

IN THIS CHAPTER, I'm going to introduce you to the benefits of understanding human behavior and explain why it's better to inspire people rather than push them. When you begin to tap into the "why" behind human behavior and what motivates people from within, I guarantee you will increase your potential for being an effective, inspirational leader. Let me start with a story about dog behavior.

When I was a kid, we had a dog—an untrained boxer named Grindle. Every day, Grindle would poop on the floor in the middle of the living room. Obviously, this behavior was frowned upon by all members of the family, mostly by my Dad. My Dad, being the person in charge, took it upon himself to correct Grindle's behavior. Now, my Dad is a wonderful person, but he's an engineer by trade and certainly not a dog trainer. He really didn't understand the first thing about dog behavior, but he was dead set on house training Grindle.

The training would go like this: On the first day, my Dad came home from work and found that Grindle had pooped on the living room floor.

My Dad grabbed Grindle and a newspaper, put Grindle's nose in the poop, hit him on the butt, said, "Bad dog!" and threw him out the back door. On the second day of training, my Dad came home and Grindle pooped on the floor. He grabbed Grindle and the paper, shoved his nose in the poop, hit him on the butt, said, "Bad dog!" and threw him out the back door. On the third day, my Dad walked in the door, Grindle pooped on the floor and jumped out the back door.

When I told this story to a friend of mine who trains dogs, she, of course, found it hysterical and wondered why anyone would try to train a dog using this method. She knew this wasn't the way dogs learned because she understood dog behavior. She went on to explain exactly why my father's methods were ridiculous and where he was making his training mistakes.

I told her that if she thought the Grindle story seemed absurd, think about people put in positions of leadership who have no knowledge of human behavior. Think of the managers who push, threaten or insult team members, then expect these same individuals to give their all and produce great results. In fact, studies show that more than 50 percent of people who quit their jobs say it's because of a bad manager. Maybe you've even worked with one or two of these types of managers in the past. These are the managers who push and micro-manage team members and then probably wonder why, when it's five in the evening, their people take off like a shot and don't look back.

Leaders have to understand human behavior or they will never experience exceptional results from the people they lead. Although human behavior might be more complicated than dog behavior, I would argue that the same fundamental principles apply: Anyone wishing to inspire team members to work together for a common goal must have an appreciation of human nature and use methods to inspire their team. Yelling or punishing team members, just like a swat with a newspaper and a nose-grinding in number two, provides no encouragement to do better. Such behavior is much more likely to create a hostile work environment where team member motivation is low and turnover is high.

THE NEUROCHEMICALS BEHIND OUR EMOTIONS

As humans, we evolved from our ancient ancestors. Most of our behaviors are embedded in DNA. When we were working to survive against predators thousands of years ago, humans needed basic physiological responses to make it through the day. Neurochemicals that drove us to run or stand and fight were essential in times of threat. We also existed as tribes, bound together to endure. There was safety in numbers, and individuals within the tribe benefited from the strengths that only come from complete trust in your team's ability to work together.

How do we tap into human nature to get results? It turns out humans are controlled by brain chemistry. Certain neurochemicals are released in response to the events taking place in our lives. The release of these neurochemicals generates a reaction in our mind that produces a feeling. Our bodies feel the impact of these released chemicals and respond to what our mind tells us to do. For example, cortisol is the chemical that is released when we are confronted with a perceived threat. Cortisol drives the "flight or fight" response, meaning we will decide to stand and fight or run away depending upon what's in front of us. In response to cortisol, our mind shuts down a bit to let our body take over. On the flip side of cortisol, we have neurochemicals that give us good feelings, like accomplishment that produces dopamine. Bonding gives us oxytocin. And a sense of feeling significant will release serotonin.

As a leader, it's important that you tap into human behavior by understanding the power of these neurochemicals and how you can make them work to inspire people.

In the next couple of sections, we are going to go over what these neurochemicals are and why we have them.

STRESS: CORTISOL

Cortisol is released in response to a perceived threat. When our ancestors were running away from a herd of mammoths to avoid being trampled, they needed to use every element of their body to get out of the way. Rational thinking is not a priority when the brain is telling you that you need to save yourself. This is the "fight or flight" response. Either get ready to stand your ground with every muscle primed for a fight or use every bit of energy to run. When cortisol is released, our heart rate goes up, our senses kick in on high alert, and our muscles tense because we are hyped up for physical action. Our natural response to stress is to kick in the cortisol.

While a surge of cortisol can be very helpful when you are escaping a burning building or running from a lion, cortisol released in the workplace in response to a perceived threat is counter-productive. More importantly, people generally do not think rationally when a lot of this neurochemical is surging through their brain. The ability to reason out of a difficult situation is really challenging when the cortisol takes over. Studies have shown that when cortisol is released, your IQ can drop by twenty points. Remember, we all see the world through our own eyes, so a perceived threat in this day and age can be very different for each of us. But the response to stress is remarkably similar: a release of cortisol—the stress neurochemical.

Here's an example of cortisol at work. I was interviewing a potential new hire over lunch. "Jane" was working for a company that had been a great source of recent new hires for me. The company had a new regional manager who had limited people skills. His team members were jumping off the ship and heading out the door at a rapid rate. Before setting up the interview, I had already conducted some background checks on Jane with team members who had worked with her. Her reviews were all very positive. Jane arrived at the interview and started telling me why she wasn't happy in her current workplace. Her issues pretty much had to do with that regional manager with the not-so-impressive people skills.

Recently, she had missed a couple of days at work due to a death in the family. She wanted to come in early, around 7 a.m., to try and catch up. Apparently, the regional manager had informed her just a few weeks before that she needed to restrict her hours to 9 a.m. to 6 p.m. because she was getting too much overtime. She had specifically been given permission from the center manager to come in at 7 a.m. however, to catch up because she was nowhere close to getting overtime that week due to the missed days. At 7:30 a.m., Jane was working at her desk when the regional manager walked in. He did not even say so much as good morning before launching into, "Why are you here so early?! I told you, your hours are 9 a.m. to 6 p.m." Then, before she had time to reply, he walked away. I stopped her at this point in the story and said, "Let me guess, when he said that, you had an immediate feeling of sickness right below the center of your rib cage."

She said, "Yeah, you're right."

"Then, I bet you felt like confronting him and putting him in his place," I said.

"Yes, you're right, again," Jane said. "And then, I had a feeling that I just wanted to get up and walk right out the door. I had to call my sister to calm me down or I would have quit on the spot."

"That's the fight or flight response caused by the neurochemical cortisol," I said.

The regional manager threatened her sense of well-being by accusing her of not following his orders. She felt like putting him in his place, fighting and/or taking flight out the door because cortisol had triggered this response. People can't help having negative feelings when certain neurochemicals are released in their brain. Their body simply responds. Likewise, you can't help feeling good when a person or event triggers a positive neurochemical release in your brain.

There are certainly times when cortisol can be helpful in the short-term to deal with a real threat, but stress that is maintained over time has a negative effect on you and your body. High blood pressure, short temper, and over-eating are all side effects of too many stress neurochemicals on a daily basis. Cortisol that is released at work when stress is high doesn't have a positive impact on the workplace or on your well-being.

REWARD: DOPAMINE

DOPAMINE IS OUR brain's way of rewarding us for a job well done. The neurochemical is released when we experience a sense of accomplishment. When we achieve a goal, dopamine spikes, and we feel a wonderful surge of joy. When our ancestors were wandering around searching for food to survive, their brain released dopamine when a food source was found. Their brain would remember this good feeling, and with hope, they'd remember how to find that food source the next time they were hungry. In essence, the brain reward helped find food, which helped with survival.

The downside of dopamine is that it can also be addictive. Short-term goals when accomplished give you a nice shot of dopamine and help you feel good. Think of those games people love to play on their phones and the thrill when they reach the next level. Dopamine also plays a big part in gambling addictions.

I had a good friend in Detroit who had a high-level executive job with a large automotive company. Rich was a very successful, solid, stand-up guy. At 52, he was diagnosed with Parkinson's disease and was forced to go on full disability. At that time, in Detroit, the casinos had recently opened. Rich was unable to drive, and one night he called and asked if I wanted to go to the casino with him. I had no clue that he had any type of gambling problem. I thought, *Sure, we will have a fun night.* Well, it just so happened to be the beginning of the month, and he had received his monthly $11,000 disability check. I had no idea what I was about to witness. Rich played roulette on two tables at once and, at one point, was up more than $6,000. No matter how many times I said, "Hey you're up, you should quit while you're ahead," he just kept playing. We stayed until he had lost the entire $11,000. Then, he begged me to drive him to another casino where a friend of his owed him $500. He proceeded to lose that as well. Watching a man I had known for years as a solid, responsible guy go down this road stuck with me.

It turned out I was witnessing a full-on dopamine overdose. You see, casinos understand dopamine highs. The gambling industry designs the games and the slot machines for the gambler to get a nice dose every time he or she pulls the handle, throws the dice, or bets on the cards. Studies have been done in which brain activity is monitored to illustrate the dopamine released when someone wins. You might be asking, "Why would you keep playing if the dopamine hit only happens when you win?" Most times, you're playing the games you lose. As luck would have it, your brain gets tricked into releasing dopamine even on the "almost" wins. Let's say you're at a slot machine. Four cherries in a row come up. You receive a payout and then you get your dopamine rush. You go back because the rush made you feel good. This time, you pull the handle and cherry one rolls up, then cherry two, then cherry three. Your brain remembers this is what happened last time and POW! It pulls the dopamine trigger. You get a release of that amazing, feel-good drug. Your body feels the surge of goodness even as that fourth cherry fails to come up and the money goes to the house instead of you.

When I watched Rich lose his entire month's disability in one night, I didn't know it was actually the drugs he was taking for Parkinson's that were driving his behavior. It wasn't until I was reading a book much later about people with Parkinson's who become compulsive gamblers that I understood. With Parkinson's, the brain loses the cells that make dopamine, so a common treatment is to give people manufactured dopamine. Studies have shown the supercharged dopamine release can drive about 14 percent of Parkinson's patients to become compulsive gamblers. This explained the mystery of my friend's behavior and further validated for me the power of neurochemistry.

Obviously, we would like the people we manage to stay focused on dopamine rewards that propel our businesses to succeed rather than the rush they might get from playing roulette or Candy Crush on their phones. One way to take advantage of the dopamine rush is to break up large jobs into smaller, defined pieces. The achievement that comes as a result of team members accomplishing a smaller task on their own can lead to a dopamine rush that propels them to complete a larger task, one step at a time. We, as leaders, can use the power of dopamine to help light the internal fire of inspiration and supercharge our team's performance.

RECOGNITION: SEROTONIN

SEROTONIN LEVELS ARE associated with a sense of happiness. In fact, the most frequently prescribed drugs for fighting depression are selective serotonin reuptake inhibitors (or SSRIs, like Prozac or Zoloft). The idea behind the drugs is that by reducing the levels of serotonin removed from your brain, the levels stay high and stimulate your "happy place." As a result, activities at work that stimulate serotonin are most likely going to bring about a much happier workforce.

One of the companies I worked for recommended weekly engagement meetings that bring everyone in the shop together to promote team involvement. I decided we needed daily engagement meetings to really emphasize a sense of connection. At the daily morning meetings, everyone gathered and we played music. I started the meeting with an uplifting story and recognizing a team member for a specific event or accomplishment. I called the recognition the daily "shout-out." It was important that the shout-out was for a specific event or accomplishment. Simply saying someone on the team was a good worker or doing a good job was too generic—it didn't result in the same emotional response. From the emotional response of the team member, I could easily see the boost that came with the recognition from the shout-out. Serotonin release was what drove that response.

When I first started the daily meetings, people were often shy about speaking up and recognizing coworkers, so I was the primary person delivering the shout-outs. Gradually though, people became more comfortable, which resulted in more and more participation from the group. These daily meetings and shout-outs then delivered a double boost of serotonin. The person giving the shout-out felt a sense of gratitude and satisfaction in acknowledging the good deed and the recipient definitely felt the recognition and feeling of importance in the group. Hence, there was serotonin all around for everyone.

TRUST: OXYTOCIN

OXYTOCIN HAS BEEN called the love drug. When we fall in love, our brains are charged with oxytocin, which is undoubtedly a great feeling. The release of oxytocin is also associated with feelings of bonding and belonging. When we work together as a team, oxytocin is the neurochemical that inspires a sense of dedication to a joint effort that can't be accomplished alone. Our ancestors knew the importance of staying together for survival. Human beings thrive through social connection and a sense of bonding. We all benefit from feeling we are part of a family or tribe, and we appreciate that most things in life are better when we can share them with people with whom we feel a bond. Creating an environment at work that favors oxytocin is thus going to inspire a spirit of collaboration, safety and trust.

While in the airport the other day, I read a leadership book that made the argument that you shouldn't hire people with the intent that you can motivate them. Instead, the author advised hiring motivated people—as if there were an entire segment of the population that had no interest in working, much less excelling at their job. I completely disagree with this idea. People intrinsically desire to be a part of an operation or team that works well together. Too often, we hire motivated people then de-motivate them by not being mindful of the work environment we've created.

As a regional manager, I've seen how important it is to create an environment for team member motivation. Here's a recent example: I had a body tech named Bob who transferred from one center in my market, where he was a good producer and a motivated, happy team member, to another store out of my area. A few months later, I received a call from the center manager where Bob was now working, wondering if I wanted Bob to transfer back.

I asked, "Why?"

He responded, "Bob is useless and he's lazy. I can't get the guy to produce."

I then met with Bob. He told me that his new manager didn't like him and didn't appreciate him and had no idea why. He said, "John, I just feel totally demoralized and unmotivated to even come to work." Bob clearly felt no connection to the team at his new center. There was certainly no oxytocin boost for Bob there. I knew Bob was a good worker, but he needed a different environment to succeed. I transferred Bob to a different center with a more motivational leader. Bob says he now feels appreciated and is back to being a happy and productive technician.

Another verified method for generating a boost of oxytocin is physical touch. A good friend of mine, Marco, owns a successful chain of body shops in Detroit. He has a big personality and an incredibly loyal team. Marco also happens to be big on hugging. He always gives me a big hug when I see him. Marco is 100 percent Italian-American and hugging comes very naturally to him. I am of German descent. Let me tell you, there are some significant differences between Italian and German families. The first time Marco hugged me, I felt pretty weird hugging another man. My family really didn't hug at all so it did not feel very natural for me. Now, I have an appreciation of the oxytocin shot that one gets from the physical connection brought on by a hug. Marco might not understand the science of the neurochemical he produces with his hugs, but one tangible outcome is a team that not only loves working with him, but also produces at a very high level.

We all love to feel oxytocin because it brings a sense of safety and security. It's in our DNA. What is critical as a leader, is to discover strategies in your shop or office that release oxytocin and enhance the intrinsic motivation of your team.

CHAPTER WRAP-UP

THINK ABOUT A recent day at work. I think we all have an experience when we felt so stressed out that we couldn't think straight. Cortisol release is at the heart of that. When cortisol is running rampant through your brain's neural connections, you are probably going to have a difficult time rationally thinking your way out of the issue.

Can you recall an experience where you felt a sense of achievement when you accomplished a task? Can you connect with that feeling? That was a dopamine reaction. How about when you look at your kids, or your Mom and Dad, or a close family member? Do you feel a sense of bonding, a warm feeling of connection? That feeling is your body's response to oxytocin.

Knowing that your own response to an accomplishment, bonding, recognition and stress is based in neurochemicals can help you appreciate your own emotions and help you become more self-aware. If you are feeling a high level of stress, remember it's probably not a good time to deal with your team members. It might be best to step away for a bit and let yourself unwind before approaching your team. Understanding human nature not only helps you manage your team members more effectively, but also helps you grasp the nature of your own emotional responses.

TRUST: A LEADER'S MOST VALUABLE COMMODITY

*"Our Chief Want Is Someone Who Will
Inspire Us to Be What We Know We
Could Be."*

RALPH WALDO EMERSON

A LEADER'S MOST valuable and fragile commodity is trust. An environment where people feel trusted and have 100 percent trust in you, their leader, is a positive place to work. Think about building a house. The foundation is the most important piece for providing the support and strength of the structure. Without a good foundation, the stability and safety of the house will be compromised. Likewise, your workplace must have a strong foundation of trust that promotes an environment where positive neurochemicals are the norm and your team feels safe. A workplace filled with mistrust often creates an atmosphere in which the negative neurochemical cortisol is the norm. People will feel stressed, fearful and disengaged. In this chapter, we will talk about:

1. The importance of earning trust,
2. How easy it is to lose that trust, and
3. Methods for building trust with your team.

THE IMPORTANCE OF EARNING TRUST

TRUST IS A commodity that is earned. Once earned, it must be maintained and protected; because it does not take a lot to lose it.

Consider this story about a friend who earned my trust, only to lose it on one notable occasion. Alan was a good buddy who shared my enthusiasm for bike riding. Alan had planned a number of bike trips for the two of us in the past, and each ride had been challenging and fun. Over time, with each trip, I developed a trust in him to lead our bike rides. So when he proposed a 43-mile bike ride in the mountains of North Carolina, I agreed and didn't ask too many details. We drove to the top of Lookout Mountain. Alan said the plan was to ride to the bottom of Lookout (five miles), then proceed 20 miles to the next mountain, ride up, come down (six miles) and then ride another seven miles to arrive back at the foot of Lookout. We would finish the ride by climbing back up Lookout mountain to our car (the last five miles).

As I said, Alan and I had ridden together many times before. I trusted him. When we set out this time, it was no different. His trips were usually well-researched and went as planned. Unfortunately, this time Alan had not done his homework. When we rode down from the second mountain, 31 miles in, we found ourselves on an unpaved, sandy road that was hilly and muddy. That next seven miles felt like the longest stretch in my bike-riding life. When finally we reached the bottom of Lookout mountain, we were running out of daylight and energy, not to mention all of our water. My faith and trust in Alan were leaving me with every stroke of my pedals.

At the foot of Lookout mountain, neither one of us had an ounce of energy to make it back up to our car. My legs had cramped from lack of water and from the unrelenting peddling. I fell over into a ditch on the side of the road screaming in pain.

Alan, my faithful leader proclaimed, "Don't worry! I'll ride up and get the car. You just stay here and don't go anywhere."

"I can't move, Alan," I said. "You don't have to worry about me going anywhere."

After about an hour of lying in the ditch, I pulled my strength together and walked to the rest area at the bottom of the mountain. There was my trusted leader, Alan, who was supposed to be riding to get our truck, lying on a park bench. I found someone to give us a ride to the top and never trusted Alan to take the lead on a bike trip again.

Even though Alan had planned five or six trips that went fine, it only took one bad experience for me to lose trust in him. If you break the trust with your team, then you will have a hard time getting it back. People are not inclined to follow someone who has lost their trust.

LOSING TRUST IN THE WORKPLACE: THE POWER OF WORDS

YOU PROBABLY WON'T be planning many bike trips for your team, so the opportunity to lose their trust over a poorly planned route might not be your primary concern. However, the concept that trust can be easily lost is important.

Time and time again, I've seen harsh words spoken in a moment of frustration negatively affect trust in a leader. It's a common and fatal leadership slip. We've all probably had moments when the cortisol is flowing and we lash out at those around us and use words we would like to take back once the cortisol settles. Unfortunately, cruel words delivered under stress can leave lasting damage. I've often shared with my team the following story about the destructive power of words.

There was a little boy who repeatedly got into trouble at school. The teacher called his Dad and said the boy was insulting other kids with his angry outbursts. The Dad took his son to their backyard, where there was a wooden fence. He said, "Son, your teacher called and said you were hurting the feelings of other kids at school. Every day when you put down another kid, I want you to come home from school and put a nail in the fence."

So, the little boy would get home from school, and on days he got into trouble for insulting his schoolmates, he would put a nail in the fence. Pretty soon, the fence was full of nails. He went to his Dad and told him he was running out of room for the nails in the fence. The Dad said, "OK, now every time you get home and you haven't talked rudely to the other kids, you get to pull out a nail."

The boy was excited and soon all of the nails were pulled out. "What now?" he asked his dad.

"Now, I will show you the lesson," his Dad said. "What do you see, son?"

"All I see are holes where the nails were."

"That's the lesson son," said the Dad. "Words are like nails. They leave a permanent impact. Even when you say you're sorry, like pulling out the nail, a hole is left behind."

The lesson that severe, poorly chosen words leave a lasting impression is particularly significant for leading. Your team members will look to you for approval and encouragement. Harsh words often do long-term damage to the team members' outlook and the trust you have won as their leader. When you find yourself caught in an emotionally charged situation, I recommend you step away and let the emotional component defuse before you address the situation.

BUILDING TRUST: COMMUNICATION

NOW THAT WE'VE discussed ways to avoid losing trust, let's focus on ways to build it. Communication between you and your team members is a vital component to building trust. People tend to focus on speaking when they think about communication, having thoughts such as, *How can I express my intent clearly when I communicate to my team?*

But remember, communication is just as much about listening as it is about speaking. Listening is the first step to being a good leader and establishing strong communication. In the words of my good friend Charlie, "You were given two ears and one mouth for a reason." Listen twice as much as you talk.

A good exercise relationship counselors recommend for improving communication with a significant other is to listen to his or her message and then repeat back what you heard and what you understood the message to be. The benefit is two-fold: First, the message being expressed is validated and second, you clear up any misunderstandings about the intent of the message. I use this tactic when I'm giving important instructions to my team. After I assign a new task, I ask the team member to repeat back what was heard so we can both confirm that the information has been communicated clearly without any misunderstandings.

Establishing good lines of communication both to and from your team will greatly improve conditions in your workplace. In my experience, a lack of communication results in team members filling in the gaps with a story in their head that is almost always framed in a negative tone. When people don't have a good grasp of the "why" behind management decisions due to poor communication, rumors can start to circulate. Soon, they take on a life of their own. Be transparent and open about your expectations and assessments for each team member to prevent speculation. Chances are, the speculation will have a negative slant to it. When your team members trust your leadership, they will come to you to address situations that make them feel uncomfortable. So listen. Open your ears before you open your mouth.

BUILDING TRUST: CONSISTENCY

CONSISTENCY PROVIDES CERTAINTY and certainty generates a feeling of safety. As a leader, particularly when you're first starting out, you're on center stage. You need to take advantage of being in the spotlight. Everyone on your team is watching to see if your actions line up with your words. This is a great opportunity for you to set small commitments and follow through on them. For example, if you say you will be at work every day at 7 a.m., be there at 7 a.m. Furthermore, set up a time and day of the week for team meetings and make certain you never miss those meetings. When your team sees your actions consistently line up with your words, you build trust.

I remember an early lesson in my career on consistency and trust-building. I had my first collision business, and I needed insurance agent referrals. I was going to the insurance agencies to introduce myself and drop off my business cards. I didn't have a consistent method, though. I would just drop off cards when I happened to be driving by. I was frustrated because I wasn't receiving any referrals. Then, I heard some great advice from an older, more experienced sales pro. He said, "John, you're doing it all wrong. First, you've got to get people to trust you." He told me that trust was built with time and consistent actions that lined up with one's words. "Nobody will trust you until they see you for at least four weeks in a row at the time you said you would be there," he said.

"And it doesn't hurt to make them happy to see you—bring some giveaways, like pens or dough-nuts."

After four weeks of going to the same places at the same time on the same day of the week, people will start to feel that you are trustworthy. When I finally built up enough trust to get that first referral, it became imperative that I delivered. If I didn't, all those weeks of work to build trust would have vanished. To be trusted, you need to be consistent *and* always follow through on the promises you make.

BUILDING TRUST: KEEPING YOUR WORD

As a new leader, you might be inclined to tell your team what they want to hear to please them. Making promises you can't keep will lead to dis-appointment that eats away at your team mem-bers' trust in you. While your intention is to be a good leader by pleasing your team, failing to fol-low through and keep your word will undermine your authority. You will lose trust instead of gain-ing it.

I know this because I've experienced it first-hand. When I first worked in a customer service role on the management side, I would tell cus-tomers what they wanted to hear, not necessarily what they needed to hear. Naturally being a people pleaser put me in some compromising positions. I remember one incident in particular with a Mercedes-Benz. A guy came in and was pushing me for an exact date on when his car would be returned to him. I made a promise to the customer that I could repair his car in three weeks. I knew that was more than enough time for the repairs. He asked, "Do I have your word on that?" and I answered, "Absolutely, I guarantee the car will be done in three weeks."

I set to work on the repair right away: I put the car in process, ordered the parts, repaired the damage, and had it painted in a timely manner. But then, and only then, did I realize during reassembly that we had the wrong headlight. Unfortunately, the correct one was on, what we in the body shop business call, "galactic back-order." Galactic back-order means you have no idea when it will be available.

The final week approached. Two days before the three-week deadline, I realized the vehicle was not going to be ready. I also realized I had made a promise to a customer that I was not going to be able to keep. I reluctantly picked up the phone to give the customer the news. I said, "I apologize, but the car will not be ready on time due to a back-ordered part."

"You gave me your word," the customer said. "You made a promise, so apparently you are not trustworthy."

I felt a pit in my stomach, and I responded, "Yes sir, I am trustworthy, but this was out of my control."

"If you knew that elements of the repair were out of your control, why did you give me your promise, your word that it would be fixed in three weeks?" he asked.

Lesson learned, the hard way. Moving forward, I was careful not to give my word unless I was absolutely certain I could honor my commitment. I had to learn to appreciate that telling people what you think they want to hear does not benefit anyone if you can't deliver on the promise. I have found this to be equally important with my team members as it is with our customers.

BUILDING TRUST: STAY ABOVE THE GOSSIP

YOU MIGHT ENCOUNTER team members who are anxious to share personal issues about others in the workplace. I refer to these types as trust-stealers, the team members looking to bait you with the gossip on their fellow teammates. Avoid workplace gossip. Don't get caught in the trap where you find yourself participating in a conversation with a team member about a fellow team member. As a leader, your job is to base your decisions on facts, not rumors. Furthermore, as soon as you make a comment about a fellow team member, you have become a co-conspirator in that rumor. You will lose trust because if your team hears you speaking about others behind their back, they will assume you also talk about them. Gossip in the workplace destroys trust.

My policy is to stop the gossipers before they get too far into their story and shift the conversation. I might say something like, "I'm sure you understand that, as a leader, my job is to foster a trusting and safe environment for everyone. To do that, I need to protect every team member and give he or she the benefit of the doubt. I'm sure you would want me to do the same if someone else were saying something negative about you."

If you lend an ear to negativity, you will contribute to the division and create a stressful workplace where team members don't feel safe. Most importantly, when you help your team work through any issues, do it with total transparency. That's how you create a trusting work environment.

INTEGRITY

INTEGRITY GOES HAND in hand with trust. I'm reminded of the time I opened my body shop in Detroit. We were losing customers to another shop across town that offered free loaner cars and waving customer deductibles. It was common knowledge that you could not provide those types of giveaways and make a profit unless you were somehow cheating the system. I remember having a discussion with my Dad about it. He gave me some advice I have always found to be true.

"Remember that the truth always surfaces," he said. "The guy across town might get away with it for little while, but it has been my experience that, if he's doing something illegal, he will get caught."

Sure enough, about nine months later the truth surfaced for my unethical competitor. As luck would have it—or unlucky in his case—a police officer took his wife's car to my competitor's body shop for some work. When the officer was on traffic duty a week later, he noticed a red Buick next to him at a light and thought, "Wow, that car looks like my wife's car, but hers is at the body shop."

When the light changed, the driver pulled away and the police officer spotted the license plate. Guess what: It was his wife's car. When he pulled the driver over, the officer discovered he had been offered the red Buick as a loaner while his car was in the shop. So much for my competitor. The community lost all trust in him and his shop was forced to close. Remember, as my Dad said, "The truth always surfaces," so act ethically and with integrity.

CHAPTER WRAP-UP

To RECAP, THE methods for generating trust from your team include:

1. Establishing open lines of communication
2. Aligning your actions with your words
3. Being consistent
4. Avoiding making promises you can't keep
5. Never engaging in office gossip

Having a team that operates with a high level of integrity also greatly benefits an overall feeling of trust in the workplace. If there is a sense that the business operation is on the shady side, then building trust among your team members will be challenging as trust and integrity go hand in hand.

One day, you might find yourself in competition with a dishonest business rival. If you lower your own standards to generate a short-term gain, chances are you will lose in the end. The potential damage you might do to that fragile trust you have worked so hard to build can disappear in a heartbeat.

CHAPTER 4
THE POWER OF WORDS

*"Every Time You Speak, You Are
Auditioning for Leadership."*

JAMES HUMES

NOW YOU HAVE some clues into what science reveals about human behavior. As humans, we are ruled by the neurochemicals in our minds that tell our bodies how to respond and, in turn, dictate how we feel. We are emotional creatures, and the release of neurochemicals is behind our feelings. So, how can we go about influencing these neurochemicals in our brains and those of the people we manage? How can we make human behavior work for us? One powerful way to do this is by putting thought into how you choose your words.

For many years, I ran my own body shops. I was the boss, and I was responsible for making the tough decisions, dealing with difficult customers, and managing all of the people who worked for me. In my mind, the job was the primary source of my stress. I told myself that it was a stressful business. How stressful? Let's put it this way: My office manager knew where to find replacement phones really quickly. I had a terrible habit of breaking the phone when I slammed it down in anger or disgust, and that happened a lot. Looking back on it today, I realize by behaving like a rodeo bull in a glass museum, whenever I became upset over something, I must have been setting the tone for a pretty hostile work environment. I was letting the cortisol rule my world. I was using the push method to motivate my team. I hadn't yet learned the secrets of being an inspirational leader.

BRING ME A JAR OF STRESS

When I left the body shop business at the age of 46, I became a personal trainer. I sought a job I thought would get me away from the daily grind and the stress associated with managing a team of people. However, I still took my job seriously because it was my job. I remember one day, early on, one of the other personal trainers at the gym told me I needed to chill out and have more fun. I started watching him. He was doing the same job I was, but he was having fun with it and earning plenty of money at the same time. I slowly started to realize I needed to change the way I thought about work, and the narrative I told myself about my job. Later, I realized I needed to change my own neurochemicals from primarily a cortisol-driven mindset to one based in serotonin.

The idea that work was serious business and a certain amount of stress went with all work, even fitness training, was programmed in me from an early age. After all, I still had to make enough money to support my family. Furthermore, I didn't want to fail at my newfound profession. In the fitness business, however, being overly serious isn't conducive to building your client base, a key for success. It dawned on me that I really had to work to develop a positive attitude. I had to be someone who my clients would want to see and train with when they walked in the gym door.

About a year later, a gym member walked up to me and said that she would like to train with me because I always looked like I was having fun and she really liked my laugh. I remember that moment as a profound personal turning point. So, how did I get there? How did I change my story about work? How did I escape the grips of cortisol?

I had started researching and reading a lot of "self-help" books. I came across many experts who promoted creating a positive attitude by down-playing emotional responses. They said things like, "Don't sweat the small stuff," and tossed out other catchphrases. The key to success was to be more clinical and rational as opposed to being overly emotional. Many of these books and life plans seemed to ignore the simple fact that we, as human beings, *are* feeling, emotional creatures. We are governed by our emotions for a good reason. We are driven by our brain chemistry. We have strong responses because, ultimately, the human brain is designed to protect us and keep us alive. Advising people to try and ignore or bury their feelings seemed to me a lot like asking someone not to breathe.

Back in those early days of being a new trainer, I remember telling my friend Ron about the pressure I felt to succeed. I gave him some examples of the types of things that were causing me stress.

"Let me ask you this, John," he said. "Can you get me a jar of stress?"

"No," I said, "Of course not, Ron. I can't get you a jar of stress."

He said, "Exactly, because stress comes from within you, your thoughts, and the story you tell yourself about the events in your life."

THE EMOTIONAL IMPACT OF WORDS

RON UNDERSTOOD VERY well that human beings are "meaning-assigning" creatures. When we encounter an event, we determine in our minds whether it is a good thing or a bad thing. If our brain places the event in the bad category, then our physiological response is the release of cortisol, after which we begin to "stress" about it.

But, here's the secret: We have a choice about the value we assign an event. We can control our response by choosing the words we use to label that event. This will probably come as no surprise, but negative words induce a bad feeling and positive words produce positive feelings. That might seem pretty obvious, but the tangible results from actually doing it will shock you.

Let's give it a try. I want you to think about the word love and connect with how that makes you feel. It probably feels good, right?

Next, I want you to think about the word hate. How does that word make you feel? Bad, right?

By understanding that our feelings are a direct product of the words we use and that those words have a direct impact on our physiology, we gain the power to control our responses through our word choices. Changing the words you use to define an event is absolutely the first step for turning a "bad" day into a better one.

A GOOD THING OR A BAD THING?

ONE OF MY favorite stories is about a young farmer who goes to plow his fields and his horse dies. Afterward, he goes to see his father and tells him what happened. His father says, "Is that a good thing or a bad thing?"

"Well, of course, it's a bad thing," the son replies. "Now, I can't plow my fields."

The next day, soldiers come to town looking to draft all the young men who own a horse. The young farmer isn't taken because he has no horse. He goes to see his father and tells him he has avoided going to war because his horse died. His father says, "Is this a good thing or a bad thing?"

"Well, of course, this is a good thing!" says the son

"If you say so, son," answers his father.

The next day a beautiful white horse shows up on the young farmer's doorstep. No one claims the horse, and the son uses the horse to plow his fields. He goes to tell his father about his good fortune. His father repeats, "Is this a good thing or a bad thing?" The son again believes it to be a good thing. Until the next day, when the general notices his beautiful white horse is missing and orders his men to track down the thief with his horse and arrest him.

Our brains really want to assign a meaning to the tasks, events and interactions that happen on a daily, hour-by-hour basis. Was that a good thing that I got stuck in traffic and now I'm late for my appointment? Most of us are going to say, no, how could that be a good thing? The reality is we never really know the outcome of such events; we just project they're going to adversely affect our day. Assigning a negative value to events of course brings on a strong surge of cortisol, which leads to a feeling of stress and impairs our ability to cope with the outcome, whether it's actually "good" or "bad." So, what can we do to help circumvent that negative feedback loop and reduce our stress?

Start by using different words to describe an event so that a "bad" incident can be converted into a situation that's going to have less of an impact on how we feel.

When I was a manager, I would explain to my team that events are going to happen. Your job is to avoid tying negative value to the events. We can't undo an event, but we can define how we deal with the aftermath. Associating an event with a negative value releases cortisol, creates stress, and limits our ability to handle the next event that will surely come along. Instead, take control of those events that happen by taking control of the story you tell yourself.

PROBLEMS AS OPPORTUNITIES

REMEMBER WHEN I told you about taking over the underperforming shop? I recall the first day. I had an endless stream of people walking into my office. Each one greeted me with either, "I have a problem" or "Let me tell you about the problem with such and such." Then, they proceeded to dump all the details right into my lap. I could feel myself getting caught up in the negativity. The cortisol was flowing. Stress was everywhere. I recognized in that moment that each person was tying a destructive emotional value to whatever issue he or she had, amplifying the problem. They were feeling bad, which led to me feeling bad, and pretty soon we were spreading ill will throughout the entire store.

By the end of the day, I was overwhelmed by the constant barrage of complaints and the general feeling of "What have I just gotten myself into?" I went home and did what I normally do—go to the gym and working out to relieve some of my own cortisol release. Like many challenges in my life, I decided it was best to sleep on it. I often find that if I go to sleep with a matter on my mind, I wake up around three in the morning with a clear idea of how to proceed. This time, I recognized I was getting caught up in the negative story that the team members in this store were telling themselves. All I had heard nonstop on my first day was negativity: problems, problems, problems. My employees believed the shop was a problem-ridden, out-of-control, mess of a place to work. I knew I had to teach my teammates about the power of words and start recasting some of those negative feelings.

The next morning, I called a team meeting. "Yesterday, I spent the entire day listening to all of your problems and recognized that it made me feel bad and it made you feel bad," I said. "That is the power of words. I want you to understand that when an event happens, we're the ones who assign the value to it. In other words, you never know if it is a good or bad thing. Going forward, we are no longer going to use the word problem; instead, we are going to use the word 'opportunity' to describe our challenges."

I then went on to have them do the exercise I just had you do: saying the word love and then the word hate to understand how different those words make one feel.

At first, the team made fun of the new phrase and many "opportunities" were bantered about. But, over time, the reframing of problems took hold. Our feelings became more positive and the mood and store morale improved dramatically.

ACCENTUATE THE POSITIVE

As a leader, we strive to create an environment where our team can feel safe, respected and valued in a positive, uplifting space. We want a place where people have serotonin, oxytocin and dopamine in excess and limit cortisol. If you are feeling overwhelmed and predict pending doom, then your team will sense your stress and insecurity.

One of the demonstrations I have done for my team is taking a glass of water and a bottle of food coloring. I place one tiny drop of food coloring in the water. Then, we watch as the entire glass takes on the color. One tiny drop of negativity in an office or workplace has the same effect—that negativity can spread and take over in a heartbeat.

When I first started as a regional manager, I was told to "sit-in" on a call being given by another, more experienced manager—let's call him Ted. Regional managers were tasked with setting up a group call with all of their managers in the region to go over their status on reaching monthly goals. I was told Ted's calls were well done and that perhaps I could pick up some pointers. Ted's call happened to fall on December 26, a day when everyone was just coming back from their holiday vacation. Ted chose to lead the call with all the negative issues he saw in his market. He went on throughout the call to talk about issues that were "making him sick to his stomach," all the problems he saw, and even problematic upcoming events he feared and dreaded might happen in his market. I thought, *Wow, feelings of insecurity and pending doom, what a way to inspire people just returning to work. Happy Holidays*—your gift from me is a big dose of cortisol! I did pick up some pointers from Ted: mainly how *not* to conduct my manager calls.

Spend a day just being conscious of your word choices. How many times do you say you will "try" to do a particular thing? Try is usually a word we use for something we don't really want to do. In the words of the Star Wars' character Yoda, "Do or do not. There is no try." Here's my challenge to you: Replace negative words like problem, try, situation, issue, disappointing, unfortunate, ugly, bad,and curse words with positive ones like opportunity, prospect, opening, do, encourage, outstanding, beautiful, good job, better and improve. This might sound simple, but I bet you'll be amazed by how transformative words can be.

CHAPTER WRAP-UP

THE WORDS YOU use on a daily basis become your habit words.

If your habit words are mostly negative, chances are your days are quite stress-filled. How do I know? Well, those were my days before I learned how the power of words can influence one's attitude and outlook on life. When I rewired my negative habit words to positive habit words, I became an upbeat, happier person who people enjoyed being with.

Leaders need to understand how to light their own internal fires first before they can light the fires of the people they lead. Start improving your outlook by becoming conscious of your words and the meaning you assign to your daily events.

LEADERSHIP, BUILDING RAPPORT, AND THE ART OF PERSUASION

"Leadership is the art of getting someone else to do something you want done because he wants to do it."

Dwight D. Eisenhower

NOW THAT YOU have an appreciation of the neurochemicals that drive behavior and the importance of building trust, let's look at some methods to help inspire your team. In this chapter, we will cover topics you can add to your toolbox to improve leadership skills. Let's start with the importance of body language, an often overlooked component for understanding human beings.

THE ORIGIN OF BODY LANGUAGE

DID YOU KNOW that body language is our primary form of communication? Studies show that 60 percent of communication is nonverbal, 30 percent is the tone of voice used, and 10 percent is actually the words used. Therefore, very little communication actually comes from the words we choose. Fascinating and somewhat surprising, right? But if we look deeper at human history, it starts to make sense.

Research has shown that humans began interacting in tribes long before the evolution of language. In a nutshell, "cavemen," or what the scientific community calls Paleolithic humans, used body and sign language to communicate and organize before they could talk to one another. Hence, we are biologically programmed to see body language as a primary indicator of our message. When I first started as a body tech, I had a manager who would literally run through the shop all day long. He never had to utter a single word to anyone about the urgency with which he wanted things done. It was obvious from his body language. Just by watching him, I could tell that time was a commodity at this place and that slow-walking tasks assigned to me were not going to fly. The manager was able to communicate his message without saying a word. Now, I'm not necessarily recommending running around all day long as a successful way to manage, or relying on a nonverbal environment, but I am advocating dictating your leadership skills by being conscious of how you hold your body and what your body language says about your leadership qualities.

When your body language reflects a feeling of defeat, like slumped shoulders and the downward cast of your head, it's practically impossible to command respect and authority in the workplace. In fact, one concern identified by social researchers today is the current obsession with cell phones, particularly among our young people. Ever notice how someone holds his or her body when staring down at the phone? Usually, the posture is slumped. The arms are centered inward. The head points down. Why would this habit and posture be a point of concern? As much as your inward feelings can be projected by your body language, habits that influence your body posture can also influence your mood.

THE IMPACT OF POSTURE AND EXPRESSION ON YOUR MOOD

A VERY INTERESTING observation came out of a study with a group of people who underwent Botox to improve their looks. During the Botox procedure, a toxin is injected into one's face and "freezes" the nerves in place. The process generates tension that smooths out the wrinkles. A side effect of the treatment is that people will lose some control of their facial muscles following the injection. Their faces are basically frozen in place by the botox. For a time, those receiving botox injections won't have complete control of their facial expressions. Here's the interesting part of the study: Those who underwent botox and had a semi-permanent smile fixed on their face actually reported a boost in their moods. Forcing people to smile, even though they might not feel particularly happy, subconsciously gave them a brighter outlook on life. This is a clear case in which physiology can influence attitude.

Body language has a real significant effect on the way we feel and the way others see us. It can "talk" to your brain and impact your mood without being aware of it.

Don't believe that body posture has a direct connection to your mind and mood? Try this. Cross your arms in front of your chest. This is a natural movement that many of us likely do at least several times a day. Are your arms crossed? Now look down and see which arm is closest to your body. Which arm is underneath and which one is on top? Got it?

Now, I want you to cross your arms the other way. Reverse the placement of your arms; force the one you normally place on top to the bottom.

How does that feel? Does your brain tell you it's unnatural? Your brain recognizes this body posture is foreign to you. Crossing your arms the "other way" gives most people a feeling of unease and even discomfort. It doesn't feel right because it goes against our natural subconscious habit.

You can definitely use body language to improve your attitude and strengthen your position at work. When you walk in the door with your head up, shoulders back, and a smile on your face as you greet your team, your body language shows positivity and starts the day on a good tone for yourself and those around you. What sort of message is sent when you walk in looking down, not making eye contact with anyone, and heading directly to your office and shutting the door? It says you don't really want to be here and don't want to talk to anyone. With a precedent like that set, why would anyone working with you want to be there either?

COMMUNICATION THROUGH BODY LANGUAGE

TRY WATCHING ONE of your favorite television shows or movies that you've seen before. But this time, watch it with the volume turned all the way down. Observe how much of the message from one character to another is conveyed through body language. Actors are trained in the art of body movement and expression. I remember doing this exercise while watching *The Honeymooners*, a television show filmed in the 1950s that you can still find on YouTube. *The Honeymooners* was one of the first "situation comedy" programs to air. Jackie Gleason, the star of the show, was a genius at his craft, and his use of body language is truly masterful. By watching a program of yours on mute, you can quickly see communication depends upon physical expression versus spoken words.

Your body language, posture and attitude don't just influence your mood. They're integral to the message you project to those around you. Having positive body language is just one element, though. You have to be observant and attentive to the language of others as well. Being able to read the body language of others is a critical aspect of dealing with your team members. When you approach someone on your team, particularly if you need to have an important discussion with them, it's crucial to note their body language. How they hold themselves and their posture will be a pretty good indication of their mood and ability to discuss an issue and be open to persuasion.

Here's an example. I had a team member who we'll call Tony. Tony had let me know that he was considering leaving our company for another. Tony was a good worker and a valued team member, so my task was to find out exactly why he was considering a change in employment and persuade him to stay. When I invited Tony into my office, he sat with his arms crossed and leaned back in his chair. I knew from his posture, arms crossed and leaning back, that he wasn't in an open place to discuss the real issues at hand. His body language was completely closed. I began to converse with him. After about 15 minutes, Tony was still sitting back with his arms crossed. My tactic was to "walk back" the conversation. I started asking him about where he went to school and what college he attended. He offered that he had attended college and then went on to earn his master of business administration. An MBA? This was news to me. "Wow!" I said to Tony. "That's impressive. I did not know you had an MBA."

Tony's mood immediately shifted, his arms uncrossed, and he began to lean forward in his chair. I could tell by his new open body posture that his entire demeanor had just changed. He was now in a more accessible place for us to have a conversation. I realized also that he had felt dis-respected at work and needed the validation that came from my response about his education. I sensed immediately that I needed to work on pro-viding Tony with job opportunities that reflected his ambition.

Chances are, I would never have had those breakthroughs if I had jumped into a discussion with arms-crossed Tony about why he was leaving. First, we had to get to a place where he was less guarded. His body language was a great indicator of that shift. Ultimately, I was able to persuade Tony to stay with us after discussing opportunities for upward promotion.

MODELING BODY LANGUAGE

One of the other jobs I had was a short stint as a car salesman. That's probably not a big shock to most of you. I wanted to be a car salesman at the time because I had a newfound appreciation for understanding human behavior. I wanted to see if I could use what I had learned about the art of rapport-building and persuasion to sell cars. So, how did I do? By my second month on the job, I had sold 28 new cars and was the top salesman at the dealership. I could transform a customer with an initial response of "I'm just looking" into a new car owner in just a few hours. Oftentimes, their response to purchasing a new car was "How did that just happen?" It happened because I used my knowledge of human behavior to build rapport and then used the art of persuasion to sell a car.

Here's one trick: A great way to build rapport with a customer or a team member is to model their body language. I would approach customers on the dealership floor and mimic their stance and posture. Mirroring body language immediately establishes a connection and a feeling of mutual agreement. Once I began the price negotiation, I would present the customer with the offer from the sales manager. The rule of the dealership was to hand over the price and not say a word. I would watch the reaction of customers through their body language. When customers looked at the price, sat back in their chair and opened their arms, I knew the deal was possible, even if their words reflected pushback. When customers folded their arms and sat back, I knew there was work to do.

With any negotiation, whether dealing with an employee or selling a car, watch for body language, which is often more indicative of true attitude than spoken words. Whenever I am talking to a team member, even in greeting or directing a daily duty, I take note of his or her body language. The same is true when I am giving a presentation. If I notice the audience is disengaged, looking around the room, fidgeting in their chairs, then I know I need to make an adjustment and use a new tactic to engage and hold their attention.

BUILDING RAPPORT THROUGH SENSORY CONNECTION

BUILDING RAPPORT WITH your team is hugely beneficial. The *Cambridge Dictionary* defines rapport as "a good understanding of someone and an ability to communicate well with them." To establish rapport, you have to get to know your team members. When I take over as a new leader of a team or add a new team member, I spend one of my most valued resources on each team member at the start: my time. People appreciate when a leader carves out time during a busy day to invest in them. Getting to know the individuals on your team will help build rapport. Team member feel valued when they are singled out for one-on-one time with their boss. Serotonin is released because they feel significant.

In addition to recognizing the team member, I'm using the time I spend with each person to figure out another important part of my rapport-building technique. I am listening closely to the words each person uses to describe events or situations. Studies show that the words a person uses will identify which one of their five senses—smell, taste, hearing, sight, or touch—they use as their primary connection to the world and those around them. Studies have shown that either hearing, sight or touch become a person's primary sense, and you can determine which one by the words they use to describe events.

About 60 percent of the population is visual, meaning they use their eyes as their primary connection to the world. You can tell if people are "visual" when they describe events using "seeing words." For example, they might say, "Did you see in the news," or they reply, "I see," when they understand a concept. They also might say, "I'll look into that" when talking about some recent interest. In general, visual people talk faster than most and tend to get over things more quickly.

An auditory person is someone who recalls information by hearing it in their head. Usually, auditory people talk slower and like to use larger words. They often respond with "sounds good" when they agree with you. They are more likely to say that they "heard" about an article in the news as opposed to visuals who "saw" the same news report. Auditory people account for about 30 percent of the population.

The rest of population, around 10 percent, are the kinesthetics. These are tactile people, and they usually make a living working with their hands. Kinesthetics recall information with words like, "my friend told me." They also can be fairly sensitive people. As a leader, it's good to be mindful of the way you approach and appreciate kinesthetics because of their feeling nature. Many technical jobs, such as body technician, attract kinesthetics. These people enjoy working with their hands and their heightened sense of touch is a great attribute for doing technical work. It may be surprising to many that roughneck-types of jobs attract feeling people to them, but it's true.

Once you mentally pick up on which language team members use as their primary connection, you can better understand how they see, hear, or feel the world. This, in turn, will give clues about how to better connect with them. If they are a visual, you can use "seeing" words to describe things. It will probably be better to write down instructions or provide a visual representation. If you sense you have an auditory team member, you can use "sound" words. It is most effective to give instructions by speaking with the person, and encouraging him or her to talk about any sources of confusion. I recommend using "feeling words" with kinesthetics, and it's probably best to physically show these team members a new process rather than through speaking or written instructions.

Remember, people like people who are similar to them. If you want to build rapport, model people's body language and use their primary sensory connection language. Team members will be more open and communicate better in return because they sense that you are more like them. It's a masterful persuasion technique that not only works well with managing a team, but also is effective when working with customers as well.

THE POWER OF LOSS IN PERSUASION

IN THE BODY shop business, we have a shortage of skilled body technicians. A combination of weak management and a man power shortage can create the perception is that a shop can't afford to lose a technician regardless of how bad his or her behavior is. This, in turn, creates an environment where the technicians feel they have the upper hand because they can go anywhere anytime and get a job. How does a manager in this environment establish a stable, sane workplace? How does a manager avoid the loss of a technician, even one who is behaving badly?

When I most recently relocated to a new region, taking over the market as a regional manager, I walked into just that type of environment in all five shops under my responsibility. Managers at the individual shops had techs who were not living the core values of the company. The technicians were being rude and disrespectful and were basically running the show. When I identified the bad behavior and discussed it with my leadership team, the managers all told me the same story: "We can't afford to lose any body technicians. We have to cater to the whims of the technicians and live with their bad behavior."

Before I explain how I dealt with that situation, let's talk about the power of the takeaway. To put it another way: the power of loss to direct human behavior. Studies show that in prehistoric days, food was often hard to find. Many times, change meant loss, and loss of food meant death. Hence, we humans are programmed to fight change and avoid loss—so much so that it takes a least five beneficial factors over one feeling of potential loss for people to make a change. In a study, one group of people was given a thousand dollars in cash and one group a thousand dollars on a credit card. The researchers found that when people spent money with the card, it produced no feelings of loss. They spent all the money much more quickly than the people who were given cash. Using cash to pay for a purchase produced a feeling of loss at every transaction because the money was gone. People never had to give up the card; it was always returned to them. Since they still had the card, they didn't fully feel the loss or register the truth that the balance, and their wealth, was going down with each transaction.

Knowing about the power of loss and the impact it has on human behavior, I set out to help my team see a new reality. One of my managers called me shortly after our meeting to tell me about a situation he had with a technician who pulled a car out into the rain before the car was primed. Not a good thing to do, by the way, if you're not in the body shop business. When the manager told him to pull it back into the shop, the technician refused. My manager called me to ask how he should handle the situation. I said, "Go out and tell the tech to lock his toolbox and leave the property now and that you will talk to him at 8 a.m. tomorrow morning. Tell him that you will let him know then if you want to keep him on your team." I told my manager to walk away after delivering that message and not to say another word to the technician.

Then, I asked my manager to think about how the technician was going to feel walking into his house in the middle of the day when he should have been at work. "Do you think he's going to sleep well with all that uncertainty?"

My manager laughed. "He probably won't sleep."

"Exactly," I said. "In the morning, do not let him open his toolbox. Have your porter tell him to report directly to your office. That will put you, the manager, in total control. Furthermore, when he sits down in your office, I want you to excuse yourself, shut the door, and let him sit for another five minutes or so. Then, when you do take a seat, let him speak first."

I told my manager that he would know if the technician was staying on his team in short order. The next morning, after following my instructions, the manager found himself sitting in his office with the technician near tears and apologizing for his bad behavior.

My advice going forward for my manager was to have the technician review the company's core values and have him sign a commitment letter stating that he understands them and if he breaks any of them, he'll be asked to leave. In chapter 7, we're going to talk more about the importance and usefulness of core values. Sure enough, the technician stayed and is one of our top producers. In fact, the very same technician now tells me that he appreciates that he works for a company that has core values and high standards.

So, why is using the power of loss so effective for persuading people? Because most people find very little comfort in change. The threat of potential loss that comes with change generally overpowers the promise of small, unknown benefits.

CHAPTER WRAP-UP

BODY LANGUAGE. USE it to improve your outlook and the leadership qualities you want to project in your workplace. Set the mood when you walk in the door by carrying yourself as a confident, engaged and happy team member. Many times, just setting the tone with your body language will improve your outlook on the day. Recognizing your team member's body language is also important especially at times when you are looking to persuade that team member.

Identify a team member's sensory connection. It's another great tool for building rapport and can be useful in persuasive situations. Using seeing words with team members who are primarily visual connectors will give you a leg up connecting with them; the same holds true for auditory and kinesthetic processors.

Finally, remember the power of loss as a major factor in people's decision-making. The power of loss is a great negotiating tool. If used correctly, it will often give you the upper hand.

CHAPTER 6

PURPOSE AND CORE VALUES: THE FRAMEWORK FOR CREATING POSITIVE NEUROCHEMICALS IN THE WORKPLACE

*"Management Is Doing Things Right;
Leadership Is Doing the Right Thing."*

PETER F. DRUCKER

U P UNTIL NOW, I have shared strategies for inspiring team members by tapping into their inner motivation through neurochemicals, trust, powerful words and building rapport. How do we transfer these ideas from individual team members to the group? First, let's discuss the importance of culture in the workplace.

"CULTURE TRUMPS STRATEGY"

HAVE YOU EVER heard the phrase "Culture trumps strategy?" Have you wondered what that means exactly? Basically, culture trumps strategy means an inspired team, connected with a common set of beliefs and values, and united with a sense of purpose, will defeat an uninspired team. This holds true even if the uninspired team has a better strategy but doesn't have a sense of purpose.

My first experience with culture trumps strategy was when I opened a body shop called Collision Direct in Detroit. Our purpose for the company was to be first in convenience and quality. We would provide convenience by offering pick up and delivery for all cars, and mobile estimating—we would come to customers so they wouldn't have to come to us. Our location was in a pretty bad area of town, but it was only six miles from a brand new Lexus dealer, which, by the way, did not have a body shop on-site. Part of my plan was to provide the Lexus dealer with amazing service, so their employees would refer customers to us when they needed body work.

The biggest hurdle for making this happen was a large multi-location body shop—let's call it Automaton Collision—that also wanted the dealership's business. Automaton was very profitable, had the very best equipment, the best locations, and a relationship with the Lexus dealer at their other location across town. What we had was almost zero money, marginal equipment, and a poor location with an unproven track record. But, you know what, we beat them and ended up with all the work from that new Lexus dealer.

The reason: My team did whatever it took to pick up and deliver cars on time. They worked long hours. And they brought the very best in terms of excellence and commitment to service. I had an engaged team with a connected set of beliefs and values focused on a common purpose of being first in convenience and quality.

Years after I sold my shop, I ran into the owner of Automaton. He knew who I was, and he told me that he still could not believe that we took that Lexus dealer from them. He said that when it happened, he was so mad he decided to drive by my shop to check us out. He said, "John, I saw that your shop was in a terrible location in an old building with a bunch of junk equipment. I remember thinking, 'This guy must really have some great people working with him to overcome all those obstacles.' He went on to say, "My guys wouldn't work that hard. We had the best of the best equipment, strategy and location, but we didn't have a team of inspired workers that you had. Hats off to you, John." Our culture trumped their strategy.

CORE VALUES

CORE VALUES ARE an excellent way to inspire culture in the workplace. Core values are the guiding principles that dictate behavior and help people understand the difference between right and wrong. As a leader, you embody those core values.

Core values empower your team and, when actively practiced, produce a level of team engagement not experienced by average teams or companies that lack defined core values. Core values give you and your team a clear direction to figure out whether your behavior or your team's is acceptable. They provide guidance for your team to make autonomous decisions. They also have a significant impact on the culture of your company. I like to say that the culture of a company is the invisible. It's that feeling you get when you interact with a place of business and its team members.

When core values are more than just a list posted on the wall, they define the culture and empower the team to work together with a common vision and purpose. If you've never worked at a place with core values, you might question their importance. I have experienced the power that comes from working with a team aligned with a common set of values.

Let's explore what core values can look like in action and examine the positive neurochemicals that are released when you and your team are committed to those core values. Below are some companies that operate with and without core values and the differences you find in team engagement, team performance and customer experience.

Zappos

Zappos is a tremendously successful online company that sells shoes, among other things. The story behind the creation of Zappos demonstrates what is possible with an absolute, nonnegotiable commitment to a strong set of core values that aligns with a company's mission, vision and purpose. Zappos was created with the purpose of delivering the very best customer service experience. Once the purpose of the company was established, the core values were laid out to support the purpose, vision and mission. In fact, Zappos is so committed to its core values that they require new hires to go through a 30-day customer service training program that extensively covers these values. On the last day of training, Zappos offers everyone the opportunity to take a $4,000 check and walk away if they feel they cannot live up to the company's core values. Think about the level of clarity, engagement and commitment a team member must have towards this united sense of purpose in order to turn down $4,000 and stay with the company.

One of the founders of the company, Tony Hsieh, tells a story about his journey. His first business was a software company he started in his basement with a few friends. The company grew as they added friends and family members to their workforce. He says when they reached about 20 team members, they ran out of people to hire through personal connections, so they were forced to hire people outside their circle.

The software company was very successful, and his workforce grew to about 200 team members. He remembers that around this point, he started hating his own company. He was unhappy because the people working for him were not aligned with his set of core values. Understanding that core values create a company's culture, he realized he had created a workplace in which he was miserable. He decided to sell his software company and set out on a new course. His mission became to help develop a company with a specific purpose to provide the very best customer service experience. This company would have a set of core values to manifest his vision and deliver on their purpose.

Zappo's Core Values

- Deliver WOW through service
- Pursue growth and learning
- Be adventurous, creative and open-minded
- Create fun and a little weirdness
- Embrace and drive change
- Build open and honest relationships with communication
- Build a positive team and family spirit
- Do more with less
- Be passionate and determined
- Be humble

Here is a story from Tony's book, *Delivering Happiness: A Path to Passion, Profits and Purpose.* One night, a group of friends were out late partying after a shoe conference. They returned to their hotel and tried to order a pepperoni pizza from room service, only to be told that the hotel kitchen closed at 11 p.m. Since it was well past that time, the group was out of luck. One of the friends suggested they call Zappos and ask if the salesperson on the line could find a pizza place at this hour that would deliver a nice hot pizza to the hotel. Now, it might seem strange to ask someone at a company that sells shoes where to find pizza, but, sure enough, the friends called Zappos. Although the salesperson was initially a little confused with the drunken request, she totally came through and found the friends a list of five pizza places nearby that were still open.

At Zappos, one of the core values is to deliver WOW through service and to be adventurous, creative and open-minded. That sales associate certainly lived those core values that night when she went out of her way to find a pizza place for people who were not even ordering shoes. The drunk friends became life-long Zappos promoters because they were so impressed with the level of service that night.

Think about the neurochemicals that likely kicked in for that Zappos team member. She got a dopamine boost when she accomplished the task of finding the open pizza places, and then she got a blast of serotonin when she delivered and helped the people on the other end of the phone. The dopamine and serotonin release that she experienced made her feel inspired, engaged and connected to a higher purpose.

Picture a company without core values just in the business of selling shoes. The call comes in and the team member says, "Sorry, can't help you; we just sell shoes." The team member certainly loses because he or she doesn't benefit from a positive neurochemical boost. The company loses because it missed an opportunity to gain a life-long customer, and it loses again because it does not provide an environment that stimulates the release of the good neurochemicals in its team members. That company is missing out on team productivity that comes with engagement. A team without a sense of common purpose or defined values has no real connection to the company, which lends itself to negative neurochemicals, minimal productivity and poor job satisfaction.

Whole Foods

At one point in my career, I set out to teach the team I was working with about the "why" behind core values. The idea was to show them a tangible example of how core values impact culture. I wanted them to feel the difference between a place with a negative versus a positive culture. The first thing I did was draw a box and tell them that today we were going to design a grocery store. The stores are basically all laid out the same way: shopping carts are at the front door, the produce, dairy and meat sections are all located on an outside wall, the middle sections are processed foods, and they all have check-out lines at the front of the store. The grocery stores all provide a similar service, too: they sell food.

We then visited a run-of-the-mill grocery store. I had them watch the engagement level of the team members in the store. Did they smile at the customers? Did they chew gum? Did they seem disengaged or engaged? I asked my team if they knew what the company's core values were. Could you tell whether the workers in this store had a sense of purpose? How did the employees in this store make you feel as a customer? What feelings were you left with as you were leaving the store? Did you feel good or did you pick up on the disengaged, negative attitude of the team members? You see, that feeling you derive from the attitude of the workers is the culture of the company.

Then, we visited Whole Foods. I pointed out the similarities to the layout of the first store, the food aisles, the frozen section, and the checkout process. Next, I showed my team the Whole Foods' core values displayed prominently on the wall in front of the checkout lines. I had them repeat the observations from the first store with the team members at Whole Foods. I remember one time we decided to order a smoothie, and the Whole Foods team member prepared the wrong size. She immediately apologized and charged us for a small size. Think about how the Whole Foods team member felt because she was empowered and trusted by her employer to live the company's core values and deliver on its purpose. She could remedy the situation, which gave her a dopamine boost. She could charge us for a small without having to consult the manager or fear being reprimanded at the end of the day. She got a serotonin boost for being empowered to do the right thing.

When we left the store, I asked my people if they felt a difference in vibe between the two stores. They all felt the positive energy from the engaged team members at Whole Foods versus the negative energy at the first store. I pointed out that the biggest difference between the two stores was the culture of the company that was reflected by the behavior of the team members with whom they interacted.

HOW TO LEAD USING CORE VALUES AND PURPOSE

IF YOU WORK for a company today that has a written set of core values and a purpose, you are one step ahead in the game. If you happen to work for a company without established core values, or you are starting your own company, then take the opportunity to determine what your company stands for and align your core values to support your company's vision, mission and purpose.

To lead using core values, you first must establish that your team knows them, understands them, and is empowered to use them. Just as importantly, you have to be 100 percent committed to the core values and only hire people who fit the value system. When necessary, you also have to fire those who don't. Every time I hire a new team member, I discuss the company's core values and our purpose in detail. I ask if they feel comfortable with our core values. Then, I ask them to give me a couple of examples of how our core values might show up in their lives. I reiterate that our core values are absolutely non-negotiable. I let them know that when we add a member to our team, we empower them to make difficult decisions with the core values as their guide. Core values are to be followed, even when nobody is watching. Finally, they are told that we will always back a team member 100 percent as long as the choices and decisions made on the job are aligned with our values. If the values are not followed, then it will result in immediate termination.

Accordingly, core values can be a useful tool when you need to let someone go from the team. Recognize that, as a leader, your responsibility is to keep your team safe in an environment where positive neurochemicals dominate. We once had a team member who was an excellent performer of his job, but his behavior toward the other team-mates in the shop was aggressive and threatening. One of our company's core values is: Do the right thing and respect one another. I sat down with the team member and had a discussion around his vio-lation of our core value of respecting one another. I let him know that going forward, if he was disre-spectful to another team member, then he would be immediately terminated. He was given one chance to improve his attitude and behavior. When it was bought to my attention that he again lost his temper with a fellow teammate, he was ter-minated on the spot.

Years ago, when I worked for myself or other companies without core values, we more than likely would have let the short-tempered team member stay on because he was such a good pro-ducer. What I failed to realize in the past was the negative impact an aggressive, threatening team member can have on the rest of the team. Back then, I had a shortsighted view that unduly weighed the nasty team member's value in pro-duction against versus the threat he imposed on his fellow employees. By allowing him to stay, I would be allowing the cortisol to flow through the shop due to the stress created by both his threatening behavior and my weak leadership. When I fired him on the spot, my team had a clear sense of certainty and confidence in my leadership because I was protecting them from a threatening environment.

As a leader, you must show an unwavering commitment to the core values. Then your team will respond with a commitment to you and your company's purpose. Your pledge to enforce the core values will create a framework for an environment full of positive neurochemicals and inspiration.

CHAPTER WRAP-UP

IN MY EXPERIENCE, the phrase "Culture Trumps Strategy" is absolutely true. When a team of people are united behind a higher purpose, they take ownership of the company. A trusted and valued team member is empowered to provide exceptional customer experience. Core values and purpose are a proven method to connect you and your team with this higher level of engagement. Think about the powerful, inspirational neurochemistry that is produced with a team of people connected through a common purpose inspired through shared values and beliefs.

ACHIEVING CONSISTENT TEAM RESULTS

"I Can Give You A Six-Word Formula For Success: Think Things Through—Then Follow Through."

Edward Rickenbacker

NOW LET'S CONSIDER how we can help our team implement consistent processes. The current company I work for has an "Owner's Manual" outlining the processes we use everyday to drive a uniform, desired outcome. In the oilfields, the company I worked for had a book of SOPs, or standard operating procedures, to be followed. The difficulty in encouraging a team to perform SOPs or regular processes on a consistent basis is one of the biggest challenges I have found. In this chapter, we will look into some of the hurdles to establishing a regime and a proven method for incorporating a process into your team's habits.

SHORT-TERM MEMORY IN DRIVING PROCESS

THE PURPOSE OF a company's "Owner's Manual" is to lay out a set of practices to be followed for a consistent customer experience. The manual provides instruction for having teams follow the same procedures on a daily/weekly basis. I can remember times when I would show my team members a certain set of tasks outlined in the Owner's Manual and made sure they knew exactly what was to be done. I'd circle back a few days or weeks later only to find the task wasn't getting accomplished on a consistent basis. My first thought was to blame the team members who weren't following through on the processes. Didn't I just tell them last week that this was the way we were going to perform a particular operation from now on? I would start to create a reality for myself that the team members were not top performers. In truth, when I dug deeper into the way the brain works, I realized that the shortcomings of short-term memory set people up for this type of failure. We aren't necessarily designed to consistently follow through.

There you are, starting off as a new manager and you hold a meeting to give out directives to your team. You feel strong and in charge. A week later, you discover that half of the directives weren't carried out or were done once but not repeated. Your first inclination may be to jump in and handle the tasks yourself because you were just recently a doer. Once you revert to doing and start adopting this behavior, you conclude that no one gets anything done but you. That's a surefire way to inhibit the growth of your business; trust me, I've done it myself.

I remember reading somewhere that 90 percent of human capital is driven to do the right thing and people are intrinsically motivated to do a good job and work hard. That article said that if you're a manager and you're not getting the desired results from 90 percent of your team, then you better take a hard look in the mirror. That's where your team's lack of performance is to blame.

Once, a group of neuroscientists got together and decided eat lunch. They went to a local restaurant and ordered from the menu. The group was impressed because there were about ten of them and the waiter was able to take each of their orders without writing them down. They were equally impressed when the waiter brought the food and delivered each lunch to the correct neuroscientist. They decided to try and press the waiter's ability. They each covered their plate with a napkin, and when the waiter returned, they asked him if he could remember what each had ordered. The waiter failed miserably. Here's the reason: Our brains are wired so that when a task is completed, we erase it. The waiter no longer needed to remember who ordered what food after it was delivered. His brain automatically cleared his ticket and opened his mind for the next task. If he didn't, his brain would have been bogged down by old information. We can be remarkably good at holding on to a thought about something we need to do until our brain considers that task complete. Then, it's erased.

Keep that in mind when giving directives to your new team. Chances are, when a task is completed, your team members will erase it. It's important to develop a method for helping your team turn a new process into a habit.

DELEGATE, TRUST, VERIFY, RECOGNIZE, REPEAT

As I MENTIONED, when a team member doesn't perform a task, it's important to resist the temptation to do the task yourself. It's also critical to avoid setting unrealistic expectations for your team members. One method I highly recommend is the strategy I call DELEGATE, TRUST, VERIFY, RECOGNIZE, REPEAT. These actions can generate positive neurochemical responses in your team members and help turn a process into a habit.

First, you DELEGATE a task. As a manager, you are now in charge of getting the "doers" to work together to make your business function smoothly. Delegating the work to your team is critical. However, for delegation to be effective, you have to trust your team members to accomplish their tasks. Make sure that your team members understand the delegated tasks and how to get them done. Then, let the team members do the jobs on their own so they can build confidence. When your team members complete the job, they will get a boost of dopamine. This is key: DELEGATE, but then TRUST your team members to carry out the tasks. The idea behind trust is to avoid micromanaging your team. The task is delegated, and then you step back to let them complete the tasks on their own. Empowered with TRUST, the team members get a shot of oxytocin, the connection neurochemical. The dopamine rush that team members will get when they successfully complete a task will inspire and engage them to do their next task. Dopamine is the accomplishment drug that inspires team members to achieve more—let it work for you.

The third action in this method is VERIFY. Since humans are hardwired to erase a task once it's completed, your team will need help incorporating tasks into habits. It's critical for you to circle back and verify that tasks are getting done on a consistent basis. A word of caution: When you go to VERIFY a task and it is not done, exhibit some level of understanding. You don't want to deliver a stressful reprimand, particularly when a new process is being implemented. Remember, when cortisol is released, the flight or fight response kicks in, which does not favor rational thought or enhance your team's learning process.

Next, RECOGNIZE team members for accomplishing the tasks. RECOGNITION for a job well done will kick in the feel-good neurochemical serotonin. Recognition can be given in the form of a one-on-one exchange or during a team meeting. Recognition that the task was completed and appreciated by others on the team will give a boost of oxytocin. Dopamine plus oxytocin with a splash of serotonin is a powerful cocktail for inspiration.

Chances are, your team members are not going to achieve the desired outcome on a regular basis until you help them make the process a habit. Here's where the fifth action comes in: REPEAT. Until a process is performed on a consistent basis, you're probably going to have to help your team. Now that you understand how our short-term memory sets us up for erasing a task after it's done, you can set more realistic goals for your team. Be patient: delegate, trust, verify, recognize and then REPEAT the process. There will be setbacks along the way, so it's up to you to stay consistent and help them establish the habit. You will get far more accomplished with an inspired, confident team able to complete tasks on their own than you will ever be able to accomplish by yourself.

REMIND YOURSELF TO VERIFY

WHEN YOU ARE a manager, you're going to have a list of things that need to be accomplished. You will delegate these tasks. Then, your mind will tell you: *nicely done—mission accomplishe*d. Appreciate that you have the same limits for your own short-term memory that your team does. Once your list is checked off, your short-term memory will want to erase those tasks and move on. It's critical to train your brain to execute step three—VERIFY. Verification is just as important as delegation and trust. Devise a method for reminding yourself to confirm that your instructions have been carried out. This is particularly important if you are trying to drive a new process at work. Why? Because your team members will complete the task and erase it from their memories. The chances of repeating the task are slim, and that's why it can be difficult to drive new processes. If you don't continue to patiently VERIFY, your team will lose the task in their short-term memory. Recognition of a well-done task, though, will help solidify your team members' behavior and make them feel good about their own abilities.

Once, we had a company policy that every customer would receive an update on his or her car twice a week. We found that the calls were not getting done, and this was leading to poor customer service ratings in our shops. The service advisors weren't being intentionally negligent about making the calls. They were just busy and hadn't incorporated the process into habit. I needed to institute a plan to verify that the task was getting done and help the service advisors organize their time. I set a time of day, 1 to 3 p.m.

every Tuesday and Thursday, for the customer "kept-informed" calls to take place. This way, I could confirm every Tuesday and Thursday that the calls were taking place at the designated time.

CHAPTER WRAP-UP

OUR BRAIN DOESN'T have room to keep track of every task we have accomplished over all our years on earth. Studies have shown that we remember a to-do task better as long as it stays incomplete. But when we finish a task, we pretty quickly forget it. The waiter could remember everyone's order until the food was delivered. Then, the waiter's brain erased the information because it wasn't needed anymore. That's why when you show a team member a new process, they understand it and they complete it. As humans, they just as quickly forget about it.

By understanding the way our brains operate, you are able to predict this behavior. However, you will have to come up with consistent training methods to overcome it. Be patient. If the task is one that you want the team member to do on a consistent basis, then you will need to DELEGATE, TRUST, VERIFY, RECOGNIZE AND REPEAT.

After a month or so of reconfirming the behavior, you will help your team member drive the process until it becomes a habit. Habits, which become part of our subconscious programming, stay on our minds much more efficiently than a one-off task.

CHAPTER 8
PUTTING IT ALL TOGETHER

*"The Growth and Development of People
Is the Highest Calling of Leadership."*

HARVEY S. FIRESTONE

I N THE PREVIOUS chapters, I've shared some techniques for using human behavior to lead an inspired team. We've talked about the power of core values and purpose for providing methods to consistently achieve exceptional team performance. In this chapter, I am going to share my real-life experience using these leadership tools to produce amazing results.

I was working for a big corporation when I received a visit from the company vice president. He explained that a manager at one of their largest centers had suddenly quit, and they needed me to transfer to that location and run the shop. The center, JMS Collision, was underperforming and had a discouraged, disengaged team in place. I will now share with you how I used the techniques in this book to turn that group into an inspired team that produced record sales and customer satisfaction in just three months.

When the vice president came to me with the offer to transfer to JMS Collision, he said, "John, after I hired you, I had a few phone calls regarding your unique leadership methods, and I would answer that you were either a complete nut or a genius. Time would tell. Thankfully for me, time has told us you're a leadership genius, and we would like to give you another opportunity to perform your magic at one of our largest centers in the company." He then told me that the shop had grown too big for the previous manager, who had lost control of the team. I accepted the offer on the spot.

When I walked in the door at JMS Collision, I could tell the place had a negative, disengaged culture. There were about fifty-five stressed-out team members. The place had terrible customer satisfaction. Team engagement was in the basement. Let's just say, from the get-go, I could feel the high levels of cortisol. There was a serious lack of oxytocin as well, and I couldn't find a sign of serotonin or dopamine anywhere.

Walking into the manager's office, I noticed a large table taking up much of the space. It was covered with papers from one end to the other—a complete mess. Scattered around the corners of the office on the floor were pieces of equipment and tools. It turned out, the previous manager didn't trust his people with these high-priced items, so he kept them all in his office. He was the only one with a key. My regional manager was sitting at the table at a place where he had cleared off enough room to put down his computer.

"Look at this office," I said. "I can tell just by looking at it that the previous manager must have been a stressed-out mess. He was obviously trying to control every aspect of his team without empowering them."

The regional manager replied, "Yep, you nailed it."

Here's the six-week program I used to turn that center around.

WEEK ONE: YOU MUST KNOW YOUR TEAM BEFORE YOU CAN LEAD YOUR TEAM

Before you can lead your team, you need to get to know your team. One of the biggest mistakes new leaders make (and I know because I have made it myself) is jumping right in on day one and start shouting out orders to immediately put out the fires in every corner. Do not, and I repeat DO NOT, involve yourself in the fires as soon as you walk in the door. The fires started and were burning before you got there. The team in place needs to handle them until you finish meeting one-on-one with every member.

Here's how it played out at JMS Collision. The regional manager called a shop meeting and introduced me as the new shop manager. I stood up and said I had heard great things about their team and was looking forward to working with them. I planned to meet with each one of them over the next few days to get to know them and also so they could get to know me.

When I met with each team member, I had two critical objectives. One was that I wanted to give them my undivided attention—no cell phone and no interruptions. Second, I made a point to talk about them as individuals and not about problems related to the shop. I first wanted to know about their dreams, goals and family. After I met with a team member, I would take a few notes on their important family details. At each meeting, I modeled their body language and made a mental note on what type of words they used to describe events in their life so I could remember whether they were a visual, auditory or kinesthetic communicator. I also did my best to write down a word association to remember their name. Here's a tip—a person's name is the most important word in their vocabulary. At JMS Collision, I had about fifty-five names to remember in pretty short-order, so word association was helpful.

Individual meetings allowed me to start building the trust I needed to lead the team and help them feel more comfortable with me. When I committed to the one-on-one meetings and followed through, I started to gain that precious leadership commodity: trust. Meeting with each team member also made them feel appreciated and recognized, which gave them a boost of serotonin. When team members left their one-on-one meeting, they felt good because I had just given them an uplifting neurochemical release.

To recap, one-on-one meetings that take place at the start are key for building trust, rapport and gathering the data you will need to understand the internal motivators for each of your teammates.

WEEK TWO: EARNING TRUST

KEEP IN MIND that, as a leader, you're the center of attention. Your team is watching even more intensely when you're the new leader in their workplace. Have you ever watched a nature show about monkeys and watched what happens when something they have never seen before is placed in their environment? At first, the monkeys have a fear-based response and are highly suspect of the new presence. They slowly investigate until they become more familiar with the new addition. It takes some time before they feel a level of comfort with this new intrusion in their living space. So it is with human beings. You're the new, unknown factor, and you just invaded their work environment. At first, everyone is going to be wary and cautious around you. You're on stage and your team is watching to find out if you can be trusted.

At JMS Collision, in those early weeks, I made sure that I was the first to arrive in the morning and the last one to leave at the end of the day. Remember, your body language needs to be consistent with a strong, stable leader. My clothes were pressed, and I looked like a leader. The team was looking to see if I walked the walk or if I was just talking the talk. I knew that this early time was critical for fast-tracking trust and certainty for my team to start believing in me. I needed them to see me as someone who deserved to be their leader.

Following through on my commitments was a nonnegotiable for getting my team to trust me. I wanted to make sure that in my effort to please and be liked, I didn't overpromise things that I was not certain I could deliver. I actively looked for opportunities I could find that were within my control to act on. The low-hanging fruit was any item that the team had been requesting, like new equipment, tools, maintenance or other capital goods. When reasonable requests were made, I would tell them I would take care of it, and I did. I also knew that squirreling away all the tools in a locked room as the previous manager had done, didn't build trust, so I put all the tools back in the shop. I had to overcome the lack of trust in the environment leftover from the previous manager. All the tools went to a central location, and I gave each technician a key. You get back what you give, and by trusting my team, I was instilling in them incentive to trust me.

I also set a schedule for a daily 7:30 a.m. kickoff meeting. A scheduled meeting is another way to build trust. Just make sure the meeting happens when you say it will. Our daily meetings brought the group together and helped set the tone in the shop. Again, the meetings were a consistent event that lent certainty and generated trust in those early weeks.

Trust your team and they will trust you.

WEEK THREE: SETTING THE TONE

IN THE THIRD week, I wanted to begin to set the tone in the shop. I continued to show a consistent message and commitment to our team meetings. By now, I had met with everyone. I knew everybody's name, and I would refer to them by name when I interacted with them. I had an idea about what I could talk about with each team member after I said hello in the morning. When you have something personal to say to your team members, they are going to feel valued. I had taken the time to know something about each of them and that was a great way to recognize people and give them a shot of serotonin.

When I started at JMS Collision, I noticed two things right away: 1) There was a lot of foul language flying around the bullpen, and 2) The team used the word "problem" constantly. You know the power of words, which we talked about in chapter 3, and the profound impact words can have on your outlook. Using negative words creates negative feelings, and we all know by now that with the negative feelings comes the release of cortisol. At the beginning of the third week, I stood up at the daily engagement meeting and said, "First of all, I want you to recognize that every word you say connects with a feeling. Right now, I want you to say the word 'problem' and I want you to notice how if makes you feel. When you say that word, does it give you that little pit in the middle of your stomach below your ribcage?" I wanted my team to appreciate the impact negative words have on their own attitude and on the feeling in the shop. I banned the word "problem" and told everyone to replace it with the word "opportunity."

I also told them that I had observed many employees using foul language. I explained to them, "All day long, events happen in the shop, but we determine the word that we assign to the events. If we assign a negative word to something, then all we're going to do is make ourselves feel worse about it. A bunch of curse words and a negative attitude are not going to change what happened after the fact. We don't have a lot of power over what happened in the past, but we do have a choice about how we control the outcome." If you can keep the attitude in a positive place, then everybody feels better about dealing with new "opportunities."

And then I said, "I would also like you to recognize that the words that you use daily will become your habit words." I then shared the following story about myself: I have a friend, Donny, who is a pastor. Awhile back, he invited me to come to his church and listen to him preach. I went to church with my family and listened to him give an awesome sermon. When it was over, Donny came over and asked me what I thought of the service. I said, "Donny, you did a hell of a job!" He gave me some kind of look and said, "What was that?" I quickly corrected and said, "A great job! You did a great job." At that moment, I was incredibly embarrassed, but I also recognized that I was using swear words on a regular basis and they had become my habit words. First of all, swear words really don't make any adults feel good when they hear them. I refer to them as low-energy words. Second, more than likely, you will use a cuss word with a team member who might be offended, or the upper management, or even worse, with one of your customers. Trust me, nothing positive comes from the subconscious use of swear words.

I told my crew that, going forward, I wanted everyone to replace the word "problem" with the word "opportunity" and to make a real effort to stop using cuss words. I appreciated that people were going to have to adjust to this new way of speaking and thinking. I had a long-time bad habit of swearing. Habits are a subconscious action. In other words, swear words will come out when you're not thinking about it. If you are somebody who uses bad words a lot, then they become your habit words and I can guarantee that they will slip out at the wrong time. I told my team that if a member slips up and happens to say problem or a cuss word, then point it out because we all need help correcting a subconscious habit. Make an effort to tell the team member that swearing is no longer used at JMS Collision to vent frustration. I ended the engagement meeting by saying, "So with that said, let's go ahead and get started on using positive words that align with our purpose and values."

People laughed about the changes for a week or two when they were correcting the problems with opportunities and pointing out the use of swear words to their teammates. After about a week, though, there was a shift in tone, and a positive energy began to take over. Just by changing the words in the center, the team felt better about their days and the team had a better handle on the fires that needed putting out. We absolutely did not stop having opportunities to deal with but the positive energy helped the whole team feel more optimistic about dealing with them on a daily basis.

WEEK FOUR: ACHIEVING
CONSISTENT TEAM RESULTS

How DID I go about building consistency with my new team? Remember talking about the words delegate, trust, verify, recognize and repeat in the last chapter? We mentioned the importance of holding your team members accountable for their designated tasks. You want your team to receive the dopamine kick that comes with an accomplishment. The trust you show in their ability empowers and triggers the release of oxytocin. The next step is to verify that the task was accomplished correctly. When I verified a task, I would sometimes find that it was not done exactly as I wanted. In these instances, I would look for the almost good in it—find what they almost did correctly. I would give kudos for the effort, and then coach team members on correctly completing the task. When team members accomplished the task to my satisfaction, I would recognize them. The recognition would deliver the serotonin boost. Finally, I would repeat and begin again with delegating the task. For a process to become consistent, it will have to become a habit and habits develop through repetition. To develop a habit, the conscious action must be consistently reinforced over and over and over. The director of consistency in your workplace is going to be the leader: you.

Being in charge of a busy center, I found I needed to come up with a strategy to remember to verify that my team was completing many of their designated tasks. The process won't work if you are not on task yourself and checking up on your team. For instance, in Chapter 7, I discussed that the service advisors (SAs) needed help implementing the task of the biweekly update calls with their customers. I knew that once a habit was created, the SAs wouldn't need assistance accomplishing their calls. To help my team form this habit, I set a reminder in my calendar so that each Tuesday and Thursday at 12:45 p.m., I would get 'poked.' Then, I'd walk over to the SAs and say, "Okay, guys, it's just about one, please make time in the next two hours to complete your update calls." I would verify throughout those two hours that all the SAs were on task. Any time somebody completed his or her calls, I would give a high-five or recognize that person for doing the task. Recognition gives a big serotonin boost. That's how you drive a consistent process.

WEEK FIVE: INSPIRING A POSITIVE CULTURE

BY WEEK FIVE, I could sense that my team had begun to trust me and that a consistent set of practices had been put into action in the shop. Our team was performing better on a daily basis. Now, I was ready to supercharge it. When I first took over JMS Collision, the production meeting was at 7:45 a.m., and the manager was usually late. Everybody had to sit in this dull atmosphere and go through every single solitary car in the shop. The meetings were boring and tedious and made everybody feel bad. What I knew going in was that culture trumps strategy. A bunch of disengaged team members get results at a snail's pace when they get results at all. I said, "Listen guys, production meetings are now going to change into engagement meetings."

I told you about engagement meetings in the second chapter when I introduced the neurochemicals. The engagement meeting was my example for generating both serotonin and oxytocin in the workplace. I told my team that engagement meetings were going to happen every day with the primary purpose of recognizing team members for accomplishments that had happened the day before. I put a music box in the shop in the team's bull pen. Everybody had access to the box. Each day, a different person had the responsibility of picking the music to play for the morning meeting. At 7:30 a.m., a team member would pull up our customer service metrics from the day before. We would recognize anyone who had a good performance measure. We would also applaud any team member who had helped a customer or a fellow team member with a shout-out.

Initially, when we started the shout-outs, I would be the one recognizing the team members. But after some encouragement, other team members in the center began to step up and start recognizing their fellow co-workers as well. The team member giving recognition felt good, the person receiving the kudos got a shot of serotonin and everyone in the group was engaged and encouraged. We were building a deeper level of team connection. A sense of togetherness and tightness within the team developed and spread the oxytocin all around. The meetings generally lasted just 15 minutes, but we would always end with our fire-up JMS Collision chant. The engagement meetings helped build a sense of teamwork and fun. Work becomes an enjoyable place when people feel like they belong to a tribe and are a valued member of that tribe.

At this point, I also looked for areas where we could improve conditions at JMS Collision. An SA's job in a body shop can be pretty stressful. The job includes initiation of customer contact, assessment of the damage to the car, and writing up an estimate based on what parts are needed and the labor associated with the repair. The average car has over 30,000 parts. When a vehicle is involved in a major accident, more than 70 of those parts will need to be replaced. Picture this: You're in charge of writing the estimate on a damaged car and you're also responsible for ordering all the necessary parts. Also picture that you have a time limit to get the estimate done and sent to the insurance company—this must happen within three hours of the car arriving at the shop. Sounds kind of stressful, doesn't it? But it gets even more stressful when you have 25 cars assigned to you. On top of that, you're in charge of keeping every customer updated every two days and interfacing with the technician in the shop to make sure the correct parts were received and the work is progressing. On top of all *that*, you're sitting in an office with constant interruptions coming from customers calling or walking in the door, your manager giving you more tasks, and the technicians checking in to let you know you ordered the wrong part and the repair is going to take even longer. Go ahead and put calling the customer with the "good news" that the car will take even longer to fix on the to-do list. You can bet that the cortisol drips all day long in this scenario, and your team's ability to reason is going down with every drop. It's no wonder the SA position in a body shop has one of the highest turnover rates.

If you make yourself aware of the factors generating the stress, then you can make changes to help reduce the cortisol from taking over. By the fifth week, I knew enough about the people and the processes to make improvements to reduce the stress levels. One change was to lower the number of cars each estimator managed. I also introduced a "gate keeper," someone in charge of fielding phone calls, walk-ins and scheduling, so that the SAs were not constantly interrupted. Truthfully, interruptions can be a major source of stress in many jobs. Did you know that if you are pulled off a task, it generally takes a person 20 minutes to get back to the place they were before the interruption? Studies show that you increase your risk of mistakes by 40 percent when you are continually interrupted as well. Constant interruptions that pull someone off task increase the workload and the time it takes to accomplish a job. By appreciating that the amount of work assigned to an advisor and the threat from constant interruptions were creating way too much cortisol, I made key adjustments in my center to reduce these stress points. With these changes, the stress levels went down and the quality of the work and team member retention went up.

WEEK SIX: CORE VALUES AND PUTTING THE RIGHT PEOPLE ON THE BUS

AFTER SIX WEEKS, JMS Collision had a completely different feel to it when you walked in the door. I decided at this point that the team was in a good place to learn about core values and purpose. The engagement meetings were a great place to introduce the core values of the company, what core values looked like, and how they could work for us as we started to execute as a team. I really wanted JMS Collision to have a feeling of family. In a successful tribe, the members protect one another and work well together for a common purpose; a set of core values can really help bring those ideas home and empower your people to act on them.

When you take over a new position, you might find that you need to hire new team members. It's key that when you go through the interview process you determine whether the new team member will align with the core values of the organization and that you involve people from all aspects of your center to help with the hiring decision. If you view your business or your workplace as a family, then inviting a new person to join your team is like inviting a new family member. A new family member is only going to feel like an integral part of the group after everyone is introduced and has an opportunity to get to know him or her. People already on the team can feel disrespected if a new family member joins the group without a stamp of approval from those already on the team.

I recommend when you're adding new hires that you recognize the importance of involving other team members in the process. Often, the entire shop isn't able to be involved in the interviewing process, depending upon the size of your operation. But at JMS Collision, I would always make sure that different positions in the shop were represented to interview a prospective team member. Then, I would have everyone who interviewed the applicant meet so they could all bring their point of view to the table for consideration. Think of what it would feel like to be a detailer in the back of the shop and be given an opportunity to be involved in the interview process. Think of the respect you might feel if you're a body technician and you're brought in to help interview a new SA. It's very empowering for your team to participate in interviewing a potential new member of the family. Furthermore, the more members of your team who connect to the new hire, the more people there will be who have a vested interest in helping that person be successful.

I like to use the analogy that a new team member is like a small seedling. Do you remember back in elementary school when you might have learned the power of the seed? You planted the seed in the rich soil, watered the seed, and took care of it everyday. You put the new plant in the window so it was exposed to proper sunlight. You protected the plant so it could take root and sprout. That's how it is with new team members. They need time to acclimate and you have to be protective of them until they develop some roots.

At our company, we found that we lose the majority of our new hires in the first six months after they sign on. The biggest reason for this loss is we do a poor job of protecting, integrating and connecting new hires to the team. After a team member has been with us over a year, the retention rate increases dramatically. After a year, team members have the opportunity to grow in the organization and put down deep roots. When the challenges come, a plant with a developed root system will weather the storm. As it is with a team member, those with a deeper connection to the team and the workplace will survive difficult situations at work. Remember the power of loss that we discussed in chapter 4? Most people won't seek change when they see benefits in their current situation. Team members who find gratification, security and growth potential in their position are very likely to stay with you. The benefits of having a stable team that works well together really can't be understated for your bottom-line and the success of your business.

CHAPTER WRAP-UP

THOSE WERE THE first six weeks at JMS Collision. In the six weeks that followed, we continued to grow and work together as a team. After three months, JMS Collision completely turned around. We were hitting our monthly mark in sales, our customer satisfaction was outstanding, and the people on the team were inspired everyday to come to work. Opportunities did not go away but the attitude of the team to take on challenges together made an incredible difference. JMS Collision was a great place to work and the core values and purpose of the company radiated throughout our culture.

Remember, you're the one responsible for creating a tribe of people connected with similar values and beliefs. When you have successfully built that environment where positive neurochemicals are the norm and where trust and collaboration thrive, you will reap the rewards of an engaged, inspired workforce. You will witness firsthand how culture trumps strategy and you will have successfully made the transition from a great doer to a great leader.

YOUR HEALTH AND FITNESS—A FINAL THOUGHT

"A Leader Is One Who Knows the Way, Goes the Way, and Shows the Way"

JOHN MAXWELL

LET'S END WITH another really important lesson I've learned: If you don't feel good, you won't be able to inspire people. A key step to becoming a successful manager and leader is to take good care of yourself. All through my twenties, I ate whatever I wanted and had a 30-inch waist with energy to burn. My focus was work and providing for my family. When I was in my thirties, it was like a switch went off. It seemed like I needed a new pair of pants every month. An unfortunate medical fact is that our metabolism changes as we age, and our thirties mark an important milestone for this change.

MY JOURNEY TO GOOD HEALTH

When I was thirty-three, I was, by many measures, a success. I was running my own body shop that was doing great business. I had a beautiful house, two high-end cars, two kids, and a brand-new baby. I should have been feeling on top of the world. But, instead, I felt pretty lousy. My day consisted of waking up, feeling pretty low in the energy department, stopping at McDonald's for a large orange juice with an egg McMuffin and hash browns, and then heading to work. Lunch was a double cheeseburger, Biggie fries, Biggie Coke and a Frosty. Don't forget my midday snack, a banana chunk Blizzard at Dairy Queen. In the evening, when I arrived home, one beer to take the edge off would turn into three or four. I wasn't sleeping well. I had no time for exercise and I was eating enough calories for a marathon runner.

At this point, I weighed over 280 pounds and I felt terrible. When I went to buy new pants, I needed a 50-inch waist. It dawned on me that I needed a serious course correction. At a visit to my doctor, I was told that I was prediabetic, had high blood pressure and was obese. I was informed that if I didn't change my lifestyle, I would not see my baby daughter graduate from high school. I had created the habits in my life that made me a sick man. When I left the doctor, I realized I needed a new set of habits to produce new, healthy results. I drove to the nearest grocery store and walked up and down the aisles searching for healthy food. I finally came across half of one aisle proclaiming to be the "health food section." This was in 1993, and my choices appeared to be limited to beans, rice and low-sodium soup (this was before Whole Foods, needless to say).

But I was committed, so I bought some beans and rice and decided right then to become a vegetarian. I drove home and I mapped a mile path through my neighborhood on my car odometer and pledged to myself to start running that mile every day. When I walked in the door with my cans of beans and rice and proclaimed to my wife that I was now a vegetarian and was running a mile every day, she looked at me like I sprouted two heads. I have followed this dietary choice for the past 25 years. Let me tell you, almost 100 percent of the hundreds of business lunches I attended while being in the body shop business, I was the only vegetarian in the room. I was the crazy vegetarian guy (who can say that?). I cannot tell you how impactful this change was on my life. When I stopped eating red meat and dessert after every meal, not only did my weight drop, but I also felt infinitely better on a daily basis.

One of my realizations has been that being a vegetarian in and of itself does not necessarily dictate a healthy diet. There are still plenty of vegetarian options that are not good for you. For example, eating french fries and a milkshake for lunch is vegetarian, but it's not going to make you feel amazing. For me, cutting out simple sugars and processed foods has been a real life-changing improvement. My diet consists primarily of greens, beans, lean protein and organic eggs. Everyone has a recipe for success when it comes to diet, and you should find the best combination that works for you. Truly, everyone can benefit from limiting simple sugars and processed food from their diet and maintaining a healthy weight. Trust me, you will feel better.

When I first started running my mile, I could not go more than a quarter of the way without walking, but I persisted. I remember for weeks I had terrible shin splints and could not walk upstairs. Remarkably, though, as I dropped the weight and became better at the run, I started feeling amazing. I headed to the gym because I realized I needed to maintain muscle in addition to my cardiovascular fitness. I remember one of the early days at my gym. I was working out with one of my coworkers, Jim Ross. Jim had been a minor league pitcher for the Detroit Tigers, and he had muscles on top of muscles. Needless to say, Jim had the physique that I was striving for. He asked me, "Would you like to look like me?" My response was, "Yes, I would." His reply was, "If you want what I got, do as I do, and you will get what I got." In hindsight, I realize how valuable these words continue to be in my life. If you are looking to attain a certain lifestyle, look or leadership quality that you envy, find a role model you can emulate. Jim began me on a path that I continue to follow that includes clean eating, weight training and cardiovascular fitness.

Nine months after I walked out of the doctor's office, I had lost eight pounds and I was running a Turkey Trot in Detroit. My pant size was down to 36 inches. I had worked up from one mile to

two and so on until I could run 6.2 miles for the
10K. One of my tricks for incorporating the habit
of exercise is that when I hear the voice in my head
telling me, "It has been long a day. I'm worn out;
let's skip the exercise today." I tell myself, "Just go
and do a little bit; I won't go hard." Inevitably,
I find that once I get going and the endorphins
kick in, I have a great workout and feel infinitely
better than when I started. The initial activation
energy for getting off the couch is the key. Getting
healthy was a life-changing event for me. I went
from feeling unempowered, stressed out and
angry to feeling in control, happy, and forgiving of
my people. I realized that feeling terrible everyday
spilled over at work and made me an ineffective
boss.

THE CONSENSUS FOR GREAT LEADERSHIP LINKED TO GOOD HEALTH

To be a successful leader, an essential require-
ment is to feel good and be at the top of your game
when you walk into the workplace. If you have low
energy and a general feeling of poor health, then
you will not feel up to meeting daily challenges or
providing leadership to your group. How can you
feel like a role model to inspire people when you
walk in every morning with a down-trodden atti-

tude and a feeling that you just need to make it through the day? A key element to my success, and I believe to anyone's success, is good health.

But don't just take my word for it. As I mentioned, I have spent a lot of time reading and researching good leadership techniques. Tony Robbins, one of the leading motivational speakers, tells a story of his own health journey. He was well over 300 pounds, felt un-empowered and out of control. He made lifestyle changes, incorporating a healthy diet and exercise, and turned his life around both personally and professionally. His book, *Awaken the Giant Within,* has sold millions of copies. In the book, *The Power of Habit*, Charles Duhigg patterns a recipe for success based on implementing exercise as a habit. The discipline you derive from consistent exercise has a ripple effect and allows you to form other healthy habits more easily. Furthermore, exercise has been shown to create neural circuits in your brain that lead to a more optimistic outlook. As a leader, a positive outlook is invaluable to help navigate the challenges of the day.

Zig Ziglar, another wonderful motivational speaker (check him out on YouTube) once told a story about a thoroughbred race horse. The story went, if you owned a thoroughbred racehorse that was worth a million dollars, would you leave him out in the pasture when it rained or snowed? No, you would build that horse a fabulous barn to live in to get out of the cold and heat. Why? Because he's worth one million dollars. Would you feed that horse the oats in the bargain bin? No, you would buy that horse the best feed available. Why? Because he's worth one million dollars. Would you let that horse stay up all night drinking beer and smoking cigarettes? NO, BECAUSE HE'S WORTH ONE MILLION DOLLARS!

Well, how much is your body worth to you? It's the only body you are going to get, and you only get the one. Treat your body like it's worth one million dollars everyday. I find it fascinating that we are all required to go to driving school, gain a learner's permit and take a test to get a driver's license. Clearly, being a capable driver is valued in our society. Yet, we have little-to-no education on how to treat our bodies. In my mind, the three components for a healthy lifestyle are diet, exercise and sleep.

DIET

As I shared in my own story, adopting a primarily vegetarian diet has been a wonderful choice for me. As all of us know, our world today is filled with diet plans and books espousing their superiority. Whether low-fat or low-carb works for you, there is no shortage of options. Finding an eating pattern that will work for you and that you can maintain for the rest of your life is what matters. Choosing an overly restrictive "diet" plan you only plan on keeping for a short amount of time is destined to fail. Even if weight is lost, the weight usually goes right back on once the diet has ended. Truly making an eating plan based on healthy choices that you enjoy without feeling deprived is the key to finding a healthy lifestyle and maintaining a healthy weight. One element just about every healthy diet has in common is the importance of limiting simple sugars and processed food. Filling our tummies with calorie-rich, nutrient-poor soft drinks and snacks is a recipe for weight gain and poor health. Limit junk food and focus on whole grains, fruits and vegetables as your go-to choices. You will be pleasantly surprised how good you feel and how much more energy you have.

If you're a regular drinker, limiting alcohol intake is also going to improve your outlook. Alcohol is a depressant, so if you're feeling stressed and out of control, chances are alcohol is not going to improve your attitude. I know for me, one beer would turn into three or four, and I would feel it the next day. I elected to replace my nightly beer-drinking habit with an exercise habit. Alcohol, for most people, will make you feel drowsy and perhaps seemingly help you fall asleep. In reality, alcohol impairs your deep sleep. While you might fall asleep more quickly, the sleep is not as restful. Exercise, on the other hand, will improve your deep sleep capability and you will wake up feeling awesome.

EXERCISE

I SPENT SIX years as a personal trainer and every year I made the most money in the first three months of the year. Why? Is there a science-based fact that says you lose weight quicker and get in shape faster at the start of the New Year? We all know people are motivated by these three words and all they represent: New Year's resolution. If you ever questioned the power of words, there is your proof, right? In fact, during my years of training, I found that the large percentage of my clients who were motivated by some external special event never stuck with it. The event, say a wedding or a reunion, would happen, and then each one would stop exercising. So much for external motivation or the traditional carrot-and-stick form of motivation. The people who trained with me for years all had intrinsic reasons for their habit of exercise and all would tell me that exercise made them feel better on a daily basis. The key to incorporating exercise, just like a healthy diet, is to make it a habit because you'll feel better and you will sleep better.

SLEEP

THERE ARE PROBABLY more impediments to a good night sleep today than ever before. We discussed alcohol being bad for a good night's rest and exercise being beneficial. Two other prevalent factors getting in the way of our sleep are caffeine and the blue light coming from our electronic devices.

When I first started working as a professional trainer, I saw clients from six in the morning until nine at night. Around six at night, I would start feeling like I needed a boost to get me to nine. I would have an "energy drink" to get me going. When I came home, I wasn't able to fall asleep and would lie there wondering how I was ever going to get up for my 6 a.m. appointment. With a little research, I found out that caffeine can stay in your system for up to six hours. No wonder I couldn't fall asleep at nine when I had a dose of caffeine at six. Everyone's metabolism is a little different, but if you are having trouble falling asleep and drink three or four cups of coffee late into the day, consider cutting back.

Another modern saboteur of a good night's sleep is the blue light that comes off our electronic devices such as our cell phones, iPads and TVs. Your normal sleep-wake schedule is based on your circadian rhythm. Evolution has conditioned our brains to see blue light as a "waking" signal to our brain because blue light comes from the sun. Your brain can be tricked into an awake state by the blue light coming from the electronic screens and make it more difficult for you to fall asleep. If you're having trouble falling asleep, consider limiting the use of your electronic devices at the end of the day. Another option is special glasses you can purchase that block the blue light.

CHAPTER WRAP-UP

To be your best, you have to feel your best. Have you ever been around a wounded animal? The animal could even be a pet dog that has been your best friend your entire life. The dog you love and pet everyday turns into a completely different animal when hurt. Your beloved, wounded dog hides in the corner and snarls when you approach. Just like animals, when we feel sick and stressed out, we don't want to be around others. We tend to lash out at the people who approach us. I hope I have convinced you by now that improving your health and fitness is critical to your success as a leader and manager. Leadership starts within you and radiates out. Take time to examine your habits and improve what you can in terms of diet, exercise and sleep. You will not be disappointed in the difference you feel when you wake up in the morning.

Made in the USA
Columbia, SC
23 December 2019

85651153R00087